MISFORTUNE & FAME

PAUL BERTON

MISFORTUNE & FAME

10 REASONS YOU DON'T WANT TO BE RICH (OR FAMOUS)

Douglas & McIntyre

Douglas and McIntyre (2013) Ltd.
P.O. Box 219, Madeira Park, BC, VON 2H0
www.douglas-mcintyre.com

Edited by Peter Norman
Indexed by Colleen Bidner
Dust jacket illustration by Heidi Berton
Text design by Dwayne Dobson
Printed and bound in Canada
Printed on 100% recycled paper

Douglas and McIntyre acknowledges the support of the Canada Council
for the Arts, the Government of Canada, and the Province of British Columbia
through the BC Arts Council.

Library and Archives Canada Cataloguing in Publication
Title: Misfortune & fame : 10 reasons you don't want to be rich (or famous) / Paul Berton.
Other titles: Misfortune and fame
Names: Berton, Paul, author.
Description: Includes bibliographical references and index.
Identifiers: Canadiana (print) 20230486479 | Canadiana (ebook) 20230486649 |
ISBN 9781771623728
   (hardcover) | ISBN 9781771623735 (EPUB)
Subjects: LCSH: Wealth. | LCSH: Wealth—Psychological aspects. | LCSH: Wealth—
   Moral and ethical aspects. | LCSH: Rich people—Psychology. | LCSH: Fame. |
   LCSH: Fame—Psychological aspects. | LCSH: Fame—Moral and ethical aspects. |
   LCSH: Celebrities—Psychology.
Classification: LCC HB835 .B47 2023 | DDC 178—dc23

CONTENTS

Riches I hold in light esteem
And Love I laugh to scorn
And lust of Fame was but a dream
That vanished with the morn—

—Emily Brontë, 1841

Introduction

My parents were rich, but I'm not sure they thought of themselves that way, at least not financially. They had eight kids, a large property and a ramshackle house that required constant repair. I know my dad worried about having enough to pay for it all. A renowned Canadian author and television personality, he was also famous, and he knew better than most how the two were connected. As an adolescent, I once lamented that being the son of a famous dad was a burden, but he had little patience for it. "Well, I could have been a notorious criminal," he replied.

Long before the internet, social media and the rise of the personal brand, he knew fame had costs *and* benefits. He tolerated the former and revelled in the latter. As his children, we also reaped those rewards, including a comfortable lifestyle, an expensive education and access to many interesting (and famous) people and ideas. In time, I realized my unease was a small price to pay. As for my father, he continued to embrace fame until his dying days, never delisting his telephone number, always happy to provide a pithy comment when a journalist called, ever eager to appear on television or radio, give a speech, support a cause, court controversy or write an op-ed article, often in the service of, as my mother would say, "selling books."

As an octogenarian pot smoker, my father agreed in the final weeks of his life to a wacky television seminar entitled "How to Roll a Joint," part of a CBC show hosted by comedian and political satirist Rick Mercer. When my mother told me about the plan, I was aghast. Selling books was one thing, but this was too much, wasn't it? It would be more than a decade before marijuana use was decriminalized in Canada. I reminded him that my children, and many of his other grandchildren, were at that time just entering their teens, and wondered aloud what effect it might have on them. Uncharacteristically (and very sweetly, I thought), he offered to cancel the shoot if I wasn't comfortable.

But I gave him my blessing. It was his life, after all, and my thirteen-year-old son (always a planner) had already announced he was going to try smoking pot when he reached high school. Ironically, the show, my father's last television appearance before he died the following month, was a hilarious romp that has become something of a cult classic on YouTube. "First of all, you need a good rolling surface," he said with a smirk, holding up two of his books. "May I suggest either *The National Dream* or my latest book, *Prisoners of the North*"?

He was perhaps the opposite of one of his contemporaries, J.D. Salinger, best known as the author of *The Catcher in the Rye*, a brash coming-of-age novel about teenage angst that stunned the world when it was published in 1951. Tens of millions of readers bought the book, Salinger's first. Seventy years later, it still sells hundreds of thousands of copies annually, a remarkable achievement. *The Catcher in the Rye* made Salinger rich—and famous. But he embraced none of it. In 1953, to escape crazed fans, persistent journalists, acclaimed filmmakers and a society that revered him, Salinger fled his home in New York City at age thirty-four to a remote area near Cornish, New Hampshire, where he lived modestly for almost six decades until he died there at ninety-one in 2010. Although he continued to write daily, he published nothing after 1965.

Salinger is often described as a recluse, but that is incorrect. He was apparently an amiable neighbour in Cornish, but he steered clear of crowds and the responsibilities that come with fame. Ironically, that only made him more mysterious, more famous and more sought-after. Much of the world remained fascinated by all things Salinger for the rest of his life, and beyond. Journalists and fans continued to lurk around Cornish in hopes of an audience with the great man. The recognition he had fought so hard for quickly became a burden. "Salinger spent ten years writing *The Catcher in the Rye*," wrote David Shields and Shane Salerno in their biography of the enigmatic author, "and the rest of his life regretting it."

Fortune and fame: Are they really what we seek?

The two are inexorably entwined, and increasingly so, for we all know by now that fame often attracts money, as well as the reverse: money often attracts fame. And fame attracts more fame, as any media star will tell you, and as celebrity couples such as Bennifer or Brangelina or TomKat will attest. And money often attracts more money, as any rich person, country club member or investment banker can confirm. So, once again:

Fame attracts money.

Money attracts fame.

Fame attracts fame.

Money attracts money.

It's not hard to see why it's all so alluring in a world that worships both, where social media can make anyone a star, where influencers with a webcam and a laptop can earn millions from companies anxious to highlight their brands, where personal security and true anonymity are increasingly elusive, where acquiring stuff is among humanity's most popular recreational activities, and where we are inundated daily with endless glimpses of the lives of the rich and famous.

I am rich. Not as rich as my parents or movie stars or investment bankers, at least financially. Still, I have more than most, and even more than I need. I worry about my finances in old age, but I'm pretty sure I can pay most of my bills next month. I am also famous. Not as famous as my father or sports icons or politicians, but because I am a journalist and author, a lot more people know me than vice versa. I get kind notes and nasty threats via mail and social media. Strangers approach me in the grocery store with praise and criticism. I don't always appreciate it, but I know it comes with the job.

Would I like to be richer?

Perhaps.

Would I like to be more famous?

Maybe.

I am tempted regularly by risky investments and occasionally even by lottery tickets. I spend too much time at work, mostly in a quest for more money. I am attracted to waterfront views and country homes, not to mention expensive wines and cheeses. I am active on social media, I accept speaking engagements, I have a website and I have written this book. And while being famous helps sell books (and everything else), the book business, alas, makes very few people wealthy, so I must be looking for something more: recognition, respect, renown, some place in history?

Why?

Could it be because we are told to seek it by our family and friends, by the media, by society and by history itself? Perhaps it is innate. After all, the cult of celebrity may have run amok in the twenty-first century, but fame has been a thing since the dawn of civilization. We all seek status, even a place in history. Once, it was celebrated warriors such as Alexander the Great or Julius Caesar or Genghis Khan. Or renowned philosophers like Aristotle or Confucius. Or notable explorers including John Cabot or Christopher Columbus, rich merchants such as Marco Polo or bankers like the Medici of Florence. Today, each of us seeks fame and fortune for our own reasons, and each of us seems to get at least fifteen minutes. TikTok stars and Instagram influencers multiply daily. Reality shows are ubiquitous. Humanity is awash in celebrity. And much of the world seems to worship extravagant living.

There is little doubt fortune can make life easier. But what makes us rich?

Curiously, most dictionaries still define rich as having a great deal of money, possessions or material wealth. But as reggae legend Bob Marley once replied to an interviewer asking about his wealth: "What do you mean, 'rich'?" When the interviewer replies "possessions" and "money in the bank," Marley asks again: "Possessions make you rich?"

Each of us, wealthy or otherwise, has a different interpretation of rich. Half the world might insist anyone simply lucky enough to be living legally in Canada or the United States or Britain is rich, and they'd be right, relatively speaking. For many, being rich is a worthwhile job or purpose in life, a warm and secure home with enough food and clothing and friends and family. For others, it's a mansion with twelve bathrooms, a collection of expensive cars and a bowling alley in the basement, or a yacht, the kind of life sold to us by lottery operators and reality TV stars. For some, being rich is an engaging, useful, happy life free of the burden of possessions.

At its heart, being rich is simply the luxury of *not being poor.*

As for fame: the paparazzi may not be outside your front door, but can you find yourself on Google? Do you use social media? If you said yes to those two questions, you have a public profile that eludes millions of others. These are, for better or worse, twenty-first century questions.

We all crave recognition. We want to be respected in the eyes of our peers, and we want those we care about to believe we are important. We want to be considered when we are alive and remembered when dead. We want to be interesting to others. We want to *matter.*

We believe fortune and fame confirm such things, but do we really want to be rich and famous? We want the best seats at the restaurant, but do we appreciate being accosted by autograph seekers once we get there? We want private planes to take us to exotic vacation locales, but do we want paparazzi photographing us on the beach when we arrive? We want journalists to take note of our triumphs, but do we want observers dissecting our tragedies?

In a wired world where everyone seems to be on television or social media, there is little doubt there are more famous people in this world than ever before, but it does not bode well. Many are blinded by wealth and drowning in hubris while others attempt to escape the celebrity they have so carefully nurtured. And the gap between rich and poor continues to expand. Ultimately, few benefit from such immoderation. Economic injustice has not been kind to civilizations. Sooner or later, it usually ends in violent redistribution or devastation. Until the cycle begins anew.

It's true that most of us would rather be rich than poor, and we mostly agree with the statement that "I'd rather be rich and unhappy than poor and unhappy," but there is ample evidence that being happy or sad does not depend on fame and fortune; often it is quite the opposite.

Philip Seymour Hoffman, an acclaimed actor who died of an accidental drug overdose, was known for his struggle with fame. "You're born with the right of anonymity," he once told an interviewer. "It's fighting against the idea that your privacy, or who you are, is not your own anymore." Celebrity, recounted the late pop star George Michael, "had taken me to the edge of madness." Movie star George Clooney once lamented the fact that he hadn't "walked in Central Park for 15 years. I'd like to."

Is a lot of money really important? Must we be famous? Is a glamorous life actually glamorous? Must we have thousands of followers on social media, only to have the internet rabble criticize us at every turn? What damage is this doing to society as a whole, to our civilization, to our planet? What does it portend for the future, and what can we do to change it?

Beyond the opulence and extravagance, there is poverty and privation. Amid the fun and frivolity, there is misery and madness. That's what this book is about.

Celebrity and Infamy

Reason No. 1 is that rich people often become famous, and that can be a problem.

Wealth has a way of attracting attention. Rich people are no more interesting than poor people, of course, and often less so. There are some famous poor people, and more than a few *infamous* poor people, but humans have a fascination with money, and the more the better, so those who have a lot of it, no matter how vapid, are predisposed to celebrity. Most rich people, even if they want to, find it difficult to hide their wealth.

In fact, revealing they're rich is sometimes the point. It affords them special treatment, admits them into rarefied spaces, and allows them to mingle socially with other rich and self-important people. Hanging out with rich people can often lead to more riches, as rich people seem to shuffle a lot of money around between themselves. And that's usually a good thing, for no matter how much money they already have, rich people can always use more (see Reason No. 4).

So even though rich people seem not to have a care in the world, most are, ironically, still worried about money, and many are concerned with what other rich people think of them. Social status ranks above everything. They want to be seen. They want to be noticed. They want people to know who they are and how much money (and power) they have. So they become famous.

In fact, people who are "famous for being famous" often get that way because they were first rich—or pretending to be. Such people are known, sometimes ironically, as "socialites," a term that bubbled up in the early part of the twentieth century and was popularized by *Time* magazine in the 1920s. It described rich people who went to parties, mostly to see and be seen, but did little else worthy of note, and it is still used today by journalists who can find no other appropriate description for rich people.

Such individuals have been around for centuries. An early example is George Bryan "Beau" Brummell, a high-society Englishman and fashion influencer who squandered a fortune in the early nineteenth century to impress wealthy friends at society get-togethers. Various rich and therefore famous members of the Astor and Vanderbilt families followed his path in the 1900s. Acquiring entry into one of their soirees was no small matter, but being rich was high on the list. Wallis Simpson, the thrice-married wife of King Edward VIII, was once labelled a socialite; so was Jackie Bouvier, who would marry John Kennedy before he became an ill-fated US president. Douglas Fairbanks Jr., an actor of some repute but less famous than his father, pushed back against the description: "I am not a socialite, though I seem to have got the reputation of being one."

One of the more remarkable celebrities of the 1960s and '70s, Zsa Zsa Gabor, was an obscure Hungarian actress until she became an American socialite and courted fame relentlessly. She was a regular on so-called society pages, talk shows and a curiously enduring

TV program called *Hollywood Squares*, featuring other people who were famous for being famous. In its 2016 obituary, CBS News described Gabor as "a spiritual matriarch to the Kardashians and other tabloid favorites, she was the original hall-of-mirrors celebrity, famous for being famous for being famous."

A more recent example is Paris Hilton, who came to our attention first as an heiress, socialite and "clubland celebrity" before transitioning into a "media personality." Not long thereafter, she parlayed that fame into a modelling career, a reality-TV show, a retailing business, singing gigs and appearance fees that sometimes reach $1 million.[1]

All that fun didn't come without a price. Sooner or later, the fame we so desire becomes a problem. The money and the fame invite scrutiny, and the next thing you know, there's a drone circling above your wedding or a telephoto lens peering through the palm fronds outside your vacation home.

Brummell soon found himself in debt and fled creditors to France, where he died penniless. The Astors and Vanderbilts eventually tired of the attention and could no longer afford to keep up appearances anyway. In time, Jacqueline Kennedy Onassis soured on the glare of the media, but could never escape it. Gabor made scandalous headlines later in life, mostly for acquiring nine husbands, and for various legal troubles, one of which ended in her being ordered by the court to perform community service, spend three days in jail and get a psychiatric evaluation.

And Hilton, after basking in the limelight as a teen, was shunning it in her twenties after being arrested for drunk driving and featured in a viral sex tape released by an ex-boyfriend. "I would be in tears every single day," said Hilton about the release of the film featuring her with then boyfriend Rick Salomon. "I didn't want to leave my house."

---

[1] All dollar amounts cited are in American dollars.

That's a problem for many famous people, whether they're facing a scandal or not: they can't leave their own homes, take the family out for dinner, or go shopping to spend all that money. Paparazzi are lurking behind the hedgerow. Overenthusiastic fans are harassing them in supermarket aisles. Cabbies have a get-rich-quick scheme, and everyone with a sob story wants a share of their alleged fortune (see Reason No. 6). The world wants a piece of them, and many of us don't seem to care that celebrities just want to be left alone to walk the dog or get a bite to eat. Even more alarming, stalkers are a constant threat, creeping around behind the likes of stars such as Gwyneth Paltrow, Jodie Foster, Taylor Swift, Lana Del Rey, Justin Bieber and Keira Knightley, to name only a few. No sooner had the dust settled from Paris Hilton's sex tape, for example, than she became the target of repeated attacks by a stalker.

Still, being housebound in a sprawling mansion isn't the same as being stuck in a modest bungalow, a tiny apartment, a tent in a downtown park or a tin shed in a shantytown. Rich people have various houses big enough to hide in, and often it is such things—their stuff—that helps make them famous. Because they can't go out like the rest of us, they build giant compounds with multiple gargantuan houses, private movie theatres and various swimming pools, playgrounds and gardens and that kind of construction activity attracts its own kind of attention, once again thrusting rich people into the public eye.

Tech billionaire Bill Gates, for example, was never one to court fame. But being the richest guy on the planet for almost two decades made that difficult, and he eventually accepted it, even embraced it. The nerdy Microsoft co-founder's profile increased when he built a sprawling lakefront "smart" house in Seattle with twenty-four bathrooms and six kitchens that generated worldwide attention. He hung out with other rich people and made high-profile purchases, like the so-called Codex Leicester, a collection of scientific writings by Leonardo da Vinci, which cost him $30 million. For much of the public, the trappings of a rich lifestyle are more interesting than software, high-tech mumbo-jumbo and antitrust laws.

So perhaps it was inevitable that things would eventually go south. Once hailed as a brilliant but ruthless technocrat, later as a thoughtful philanthropist and finally as a visionary apostle for vaccinations, Gates emerged in 2021 following his divorce as a leering adulterer who made inappropriate advances toward female employees and hung around with child sex trafficker Jeffrey Epstein. "His image as a goofy do-gooder came crashing down," reported the *New Republic*. "The shine has come off Gates—he's no longer a public health wizard, fighting to rescue the planet. He's just another creepy rich guy."

Like Gates, Jeff Bezos, the brainy founder of Amazon who overtook Gates as the world's richest man in 2017, never sought the spotlight initially, and often even tried to avoid it. "For years," wrote the *New York Times*, "Mr. Bezos did not seem like the kind of chief executive who craved rock-star status." But sooner or later, as the money rolled in, it apparently became pointless, and Bezos started to revel in it, buying a house in Beverly Hills, throwing Hollywood parties and hanging out with movie stars such as Matt Damon. He was even able to finagle a bit part for himself as a nameless Starfleet officer in the 2016 movie *Star Trek Beyond*.

But by 2019, after he and his wife announced they were divorcing, he famously stared down a sex scandal of his own. In an online article, he accused the publishers of the *National Enquirer* of "extortion and blackmail" after the tabloid indicated it would print intimate texts and a "below-the-belt selfie" he shared with his girlfriend. "People who have worked closely with Mr. Bezos," reported the *New York Times*, "have watched dumbfounded that a man famous for being a vault of discretion could end up, as one of them put it, in the middle of such a 'clown show.'"

And then there's Mark Zuckerberg, the boyish founder of Facebook, who was the unwilling subject of a major motion picture, *The Social Network,* about him and his famous company, much of it unflattering and parts of it fictional. Despite this, Zuckerberg, too, eventually embraced celebrity, perhaps in an attempt to recast himself as the "good guy" he stated he would like to be. Or possibly because when you have so much money and so much influence, fame is inevitable and might as well be embraced.

Maybe that's why he took time out from his busy schedule to appear on *Saturday Night Live* and voice himself on *The Simpsons.* Or agreed to a friendly interview with his wife on CBS *This Morning,* later described—preposterously—online as "The Zuckerbergs are a lot like you and I." None of it seems to have worked. Although he is acknowledged as a brilliant innovator and a committed philanthropist, Zuckerberg's appearances in the media today are rarely the kind that makes him look like a "good guy." *The New Republic,* for example, labelled him "2021 Scoundrel of the Year," because he is, among other things, an "amoral and incurious capitalist posing as a visionary optimist."

Inevitably, rich people become celebrities, and celebrities lose control of the fame they have so carefully nurtured. Sooner or later, it all comes crashing down. The star system developed by movie studios in the 1930s is long gone. These matters are no longer meticulously orchestrated—even invented—by powerful studios and all-knowing publicists who once controlled messages, protected individual privacy, manipulated journalists and squelched dark secrets. Gone are many of the protections the studio system offered to those with marquee names.

Today, unpleasant and unflattering stories spin out of control in a vortex of paparazzi, YouTube creators, TikTok influencers, late-night talk-show hosts, investigative journalists, random citizens with a cellphone camera and the public at large—all fascinated by the lives of the rich and famous. Someone wants to write a tell-all biography. Another is an old schoolmate with an embarrassing photograph. And there always seems to be a disgruntled police officer who knows about a drunken incident.

Modern celebrity—gossip, autograph seekers, groupies and stalkers—has thrived since the eighteenth century, but modern celebrity culture can be traced primarily to Sarah Bernhardt, an actor at the turn of the nineteenth century and the "central character" of *The Drama of Celebrity*, a book by Sharon Marcus. "No mere product of modern celebrity culture," writes Marcus, "Bernhardt also helped to produce it." Shrewd, wily and pioneering in her efforts to attract attention, she made herself impossible to ignore, setting a standard that still reverberates.

A century later, stardom continues to evolve, as entertainment journalist Owen Gleiberman wrote in 2003 in a review in *Entertainment Weekly* of the film *Gigli*, starring Jennifer Lopez and Ben Affleck: "We have now entered the first movie era in which celebrity is threatening to eclipse stardom. You may think that those two words mean the same thing, yet the distinction used to be vital. Stars, those gods of the earth, enthrall and entrance; celebrities merely intrigue. Stars have magic; celebrities require only fame."

All that power, fame and money that rich people wield so casually, however, inevitably becomes a problem in the face of a voracious media and hungry public digging for dirt. For each of us, famous or not, is bound to say something stupid on social media sooner or later. We just can't help it. The only difference for poor people is that nobody cares what they say or do; people listen to rich people. What begins in such triumph so often ends in tragedy.

Take the case of British heiress Petra Ecclestone: when the socialite and fashion model married playboy financier James Stunt in 2011, the family seemed happy to discuss the details of the lavish £12-million extravaganza. "I don't care how much the wedding cost," said her mom, Slavica, a former model. "It was worth every penny because it made my daughter happy. Who cares about money?" Ecclestone's billionaire dad, Bernie, the diminutive Formula 1 racing tycoon, was equally frank (if not as enthusiastic) about the cost, which included renting an Italian castle and serving wine at £4,000 a bottle. "When it was suggested how much they would be spending on drinks, I thought it was absurd and I managed to upset my daughter and my wife."

Even as the fairy-tale marriage began to disintegrate in 2018, some family members were willing to share details. Stunt, by then described as a drug abuser and gambling addict, gave an interview with *Tatler* magazine during which he said he lost his "public standing" by marrying a "C-List celebrity's daughter" and called his in-laws "that dwarf" and "Lady Macbeth." Petra, said Stunt, was now "this girl who's had a lobotomy and gone to Jonestown. This is a horrible human being."

Petra's sister Tamara hit back on Instagram: "Unless he stops telling lies about my family we will have to start telling the truth about him." By the time the paparazzi descended to learn details about how the vast riches would be divided, Stunt was less keen to discuss his affairs, and uttered a familiar plea: "I hope the press respect our privacy now."

While such endings are often unavoidable, most rich people are in denial until it's too late. Or perhaps they accept the costs from the beginning. After all, some realize many roads to riches are accessible only after acquiring fame. This is true of artists, athletes, authors and actors, among others. Many Hollywood stars, for example, have real talent, some work hard, and others simply get lucky. But they all know that, talented or not, their fame allows them to collect bigger paycheques and more work than mere journeyman actors, no matter how good they are. Even the already-

famous must constantly polish their waxing and waning reputations to sell product or expose their art to a wider audience, or
simply to maintain their fan base and their fame.

So the famous and unknown alike make blockbuster movies
rather than toil on the stage. Or agree to wear ridiculous super-
hero costumes in big studio franchises instead of practising their
craft in independent art films. And they go to tiresome red-carpet
events and dull press junkets to get recognition for themselves and
their work. Everyone is trying to make a living, and fame often
smooths the way—at least for a while. Eventually, it returns like
a nasty boomerang. Burt Reynolds, the biggest movie star of the
1970s, was merely a busy actor when he famously agreed to appear
naked in *Cosmopolitan* in 1972. Suddenly, he said, "standing ovations
turned into burlesque show hoots and catcalls. They cared more
about my pubes than they did the play." Years later, he regretted the
publicity stunt and resented much of the media attention.

Talent alone won't work for star athletes either. They must train
hard to stay in the game, but they are not going to command those
huge signing bonuses and endorsement deals without first courting
fans and the media, burnishing their personal brands and staying
top-of-mind in the fickle public consciousness. US Olympic gold
medallist Lindsey Vonn, one of the most successful alpine skiers
of all time, made millions on the slopes. But skiing alone won't
finance a rich-and-famous lifestyle. You need help from the likes
of Red Bull, Procter & Gamble and Under Armour, and to acquire
that, you must be famous, and to be famous, you must sell yourself.
It was only a matter of time before she was the subject of headlines
like this: "15 Photos of Lindsey Vonn When She Thought Nobody
Was Looking."

Male athletes are paid exorbitant sums to play various sports,
but that is often not enough. They need to sustain their expensive
lifestyles long past early retirement, which often means becoming

more famous after they retire. Basketball legend Michael Jordan got rich and famous racking up points for the Chicago Bulls and the Washington Wizards, earning more than $80 million over the course of his playing career. That might seem like an absolute fortune to some, but it was pocket change compared with what he translated his celebrity into by endorsing stuff after retiring from the game. Jordan became the highest-paid athlete in history and is now worth perhaps $2 billion.

Inevitably, though, the press and public begin to look for problems, real or imagined. A notorious gambler, Jordan was dogged by questions from the media about his betting, and theories about how it might have affected his career. "I do not have a problem," he said. "I enjoy gambling. Soon, whenever I walk away from this game, I think that's the only thing that people are gonna say was a bad thing about Michael Jordan."

Golfing phenom Tiger Woods is second only to Jordan in endorsement income, at $1.5 billion, a goodly portion of which went to his wife after they split, when sordid details of his serial adultery were shared in excruciating detail with a mesmerized world. Woods's wife, Elin Nordegren, recalled reluctantly falling in love with a rich and famous person: "I had my opinion about celebrities," she later reflected. "Money can't buy happiness, or put my family back together" (see Reason No. 10).

Musicians, too, require natural talent and long hours of practice, but no matter how catchy the tune or poetic the lyrics, few are going to listen if the artist can't make some kind of a splash first. They must talk up the tunes, the lyrics and the meaning of life, sit for repetitive interviews with ill-informed journalists, go on contrived talk shows, and stage gruelling tours—often with outrageous antics—in every corner of the globe.

It's all in the name of fame, fans and more money—but it comes with a cost. "The road will kill you," warned songwriter Robbie

Robertson of the Band in filmmaker Martin Scorsese's historic documentary *The Last Waltz.* Even worse, interacting with fans can be dangerous, as hard-rocking singer Axl Rose and cadaverous Rolling Stones guitarist Keith Richards can attest. They are among the many rock stars who have tussled with unruly spectators at concerts and with fans on the street. After all is said and done, the hard-won admirers so assiduously acquired over many performances often end up drowning out the music with frenzied screaming or by generally becoming nuisances. Hindu spiritualist and late Beatle George Harrison once summed up what some aging rockers only realize too late: "I'd rather be a musician than a rock star."

Countless others, meanwhile, realize they lose their ability to meet others, make lasting friendships or find love due to the pressures of their own prominence. Trying to get married discreetly while rich and famous may be the most stressful, and the results are often disastrous. Groundbreaking pop star Madonna, a pioneer of publicity stunts, was the unwilling focus of TV cameras after helicopters drowned out her wedding vows to Sean Penn in Malibu in 1985. She gave them the finger as cameras rolled and the entire debacle played out for a global audience.

Jennifer Lopez said overexposure was responsible for the disintegration of her famous first relationship with Ben Affleck, the initial indication of which came when they postponed their wedding in 2003. "Due to the excessive media attention surrounding our wedding, we have decided to postpone the date," the couple said in a joint statement. "When we found ourselves seriously contemplating hiring three separate 'decoy brides' at three different locations, we realized that something was awry."

The problem has only worsened since. "Celebrity weddings appear to be everyone's business," according to a 2017 BBC News article, following reports that famously shy actor Jessica Chastain's nuptials were "gatecrashed—by a helicopter and a long lens." It doesn't seem to matter how far away rich and famous couples travel, how remote the tropical island, or how obscure the location, the media will find them.

You can never have enough security to keep the paparazzi at bay once they arrive. Groundwork is key if you don't want your big day to be memorialized in the tabloids or social media, say experts. That's why wedding planners sign non-disclosure agreements, and why invited guests are often obliged to give up their mobile phones before entry. Guests invited to the marriage of ubiquitous celebrity Jennifer Aniston and actor Justin Theroux were told it was a birthday party. Those invited to the wedding of Jessica Biel and Justin Timberlake in Italy were informed it was just a get-together, but various news outlets announced the ceremony before the big day. Marcy Blum, a planner of various celebrity weddings, including one for basketball great LeBron James in 2013, says stealth is key: "There's no midpoint: It's absolute secrecy, or it's everywhere."

And yet the quest for fame continues, and is even accelerating. Social media and reality TV allow almost everyone a chance for fifteen minutes of fame, and many are using it to launch careers as influencers, business magnates and TV stars. Few fully grasp the consequences that inevitably await.

Take, as just one example, the story of Kaitlyn Siragusa. She's a Houston, Texas, streaming star who goes by the name of Amouranth on the platform Twitch, a place where people livestream themselves doing various things like playing video games, cooking or simply commenting on life. Wearing a bikini, Siragusa often streams from an inflatable hot tub in her house. She has five million followers and makes more than $100,000 per month from her fans, who watch advertisements, make donations or pay about $5 per month to subscribe.

But the success comes at a cost. Social media stars are regularly stalked and harassed by fans and critics. One man flew from Estonia to meet Siragusa in person; she called the police when he arrived. Since finding celebrity, she has bought guns and a guard dog, and installed security cameras. "I don't know what else to do at this point, besides build a moat with crocodiles."

The Twitch star known as DizzyKitten to 680,000 followers was stalked in 2018 by a man who travelled from Washington State to see her in Arkansas. He was sent to a psychiatric hospital; she went to therapy, took lessons in how to handle a gun and moved to a gated community.

In 2020, a crazed fan arrived at the home of Ava Majury, fifteen, a TikTok star with more than a million followers, and used his shotgun to blast open the front door. Ava's dad, a retired police officer, shot him dead. The ordeal rattled the family, to say nothing of Ava, who considered shutting the whole operation down: "I'd think, 'I don't want to do this anymore.'" Then she reconsidered. "I thought of all the benefits."

Followers, influence, income.

Money, recognition, relevance.

We want it all—or do we?

For if the kind of attention directed at some social media stars from adoring fans is that alarming, imagine what might await those who are the targets of ubiquitous online haters. Psychologists long ago recognized the unhealthy obsession that some fans have with famous people and termed it a "parasocial relationship." Movie stars and TV anchors have dealt with it for decades, but teenaged social-media phenomena are likely not as well-equipped to handle —or weather—that kind of attention.

Today, famous politicians such as former US House of Representatives leader Nancy Pelosi are stalked by haters. One broke into her home in 2022 and beat her husband with a hammer. Adoring fans are one thing, but deranged critics are another. In this instance, it was predictably followed by the usual expressions of outrage from politicians, but also by sinister conspiracy theories that Pelosi knew his attacker, that male prostitution was involved, or that the attack was somehow staged, all of which were amplified on social media.

And what happens when it all inevitably ends? For while acquiring fame can often be an uphill battle, notoriety usually comes with downhill speed. The case of Katherine Heigl illustrates the point. She was once the darling of Hollywood, an Emmy Award–winning actress for her role on TV's *Grey's Anatomy* and the star of a variety of successful romantic comedies on the big screen such as *Knocked Up*.

I haven't seen *Grey's Anatomy*, nor have I watched any of her movies, but somehow over the last decade I have become aware of Heigl's career—or apparent lack thereof, the result, allegedly, of her reputation for being difficult to work with. To me, and many others, she is famous today not for her many obvious successes, but for the fact that she isn't more successful, a matter of fact somehow highlighted with surprising regularity by clickbait ads on the internet. The slump, after all, is often more compelling than run-of-the-mill success. But Heigl is still young. No doubt she's due for a miraculous comeback, which are almost as compelling as slumps. Many actors—Richard Gere, John Travolta, Brendan Fraser—faced perceived downturns that may become mere footnotes in obituaries listing their many successes.

Others are not so lucky. Fame fades gradually, but infamy can last a lifetime. For such people, it's often a one-way trip. Jet-setting tech executive Elizabeth Holmes learned that painfully during the years after she founded Theranos, a California health-technology company that raised $9 billion before it was exposed as a fraud. Holmes founded the company in 2003, raised $6 million by 2004 and a decade later was on the covers of the *New York Times* style magazine, as well as *Fortune* and *Forbes*, which declared her the youngest self-made billionaire in 2014. Hailed as a genius, she travelled on private jets with a retinue of bodyguards and chauffeurs and assistants. She wooed influential board members, including a former US secretary of state, former and future secretaries of defence, former senators, admirals and CEOs. She attracted rich investors such as Rupert Murdoch and the Walton family. She carefully crafted her persona, employing a deep voice to sound authoritative and adopting a studied wardrobe. She gave TED talks and media interviews.

Then it all came tumbling down when journalist John Carreyrou of the *Wall Street Journal* started asking difficult questions about the company's remarkable blood-testing technology, which turned out to be blatantly unremarkable. Investors lost all their money, the vaunted board members appeared to have been asleep at the switch, and Holmes faced a media storm and criminal charges. Ultimately, the woman once hailed as a biotechnology mastermind portrayed herself in court as an ambitious and naive victim who said she was betrayed and abused—in business and in life—by her boyfriend, the company's chief operating officer. She was convicted of fraud and sentenced to a decade in prison.

Not everyone seeks the spotlight to get rich; some bankers, for example, do their best to avoid it. They do not need to be famous to get rich. And getting rich does not usually make them famous. For many, it's the best of both worlds. They fly under the radar, making millions while shuffling other people's money around, inventing complicated investment vehicles and "creating wealth."

Sometimes, they deign to mingle with the elite at economic forums in European ski resorts or are tempted by glamour. Once in a while, they appear at a Senate committee in Washington, expounding on the value of free markets and railing on about government red tape. Rarely, they emerge as philanthropists and make high-profile charitable donations.

But most of the time they live their lives in quiet splendour with other rich people. That was the case with Richard Fuld, who ran the Wall Street investment bank Lehman Brothers in the first decade of the twenty-first century. Until 2007, his life of luxury, which included a mansion in Florida, a sprawling home in Connecticut, a Park Avenue apartment in New York, and a seventy-one-acre estate in Sun Valley, Idaho, was known only to him and his rich circle of friends and colleagues. It was all good. Then Lehman Brothers went bankrupt in 2008, after it paid him almost half a billion dollars to run the place over the previous seven years.

It was the early stages of the world financial crisis, and Fuld was now infamous. A sometimes menacing figure nicknamed "The Gorilla" and once labelled "Mr. Wall Street," Fuld said Lehman's demise was the fault of government, regulators and unfounded rumours, but accepted little of the blame himself. *Time* magazine put him on its list of "25 People to Blame for the Financial Crisis" and CNN named him among its "Ten Most Wanted: Culprits of the Collapse." Shortly after the disaster, he put the Florida mansion in his wife's name.

Likewise, insurance executive Joseph Cassano took home about $40 million a year while quietly running AIG Financial Products. When its parent company, American International Group, the world's largest insurer, suffered a $99 billion loss in 2008, Cassano was blamed for much of it and shown the door. US taxpayers were forced to pony up $85 billion to bail out the company. What the public didn't know was that Cassano was still on the payroll six months later as a consultant, earning $1 million a month to help them through the very crisis he led them into.

When the misadventure hit the public airwaves, infamy arrived fast and furious. *Rolling Stone* magazine labelled Cassano

"Patient Zero for the Global Economic Meltdown" and *Vanity Fair* called him "The Man Who Crashed the World." His employees called him a bully who created a culture of fear at the company that helped lead to its downfall. When reporters descended on his posh townhouse in London's fashionable Knightsbridge neighbourhood, he had no comment. When the US Securities and Exchange Commission questioned him in 2009, he invoked the Fifth Amendment more than two hundred times. In 2010, the US Justice Department launched an investigation: Were Cassano's actions criminal, or just stupid? No charges were laid, and Cassano retreated to his home in Westport, Connecticut, where he tried to live a low-key life and avoid journalists. Like many of the so-called villains from the economic disaster, who took their hundreds of millions and walked away to disgruntled retirement, he has rarely if ever uttered a word about it since, writing to one journalist a familiar note: "I am requesting, with hopeful appreciation, you allow me my privacy."

Professional spokespeople, those talking heads who make their living as the public face of an organization, are rarely afforded such considerations. These are the ones rich people pay (usually handsomely) to be famous for them—because everybody who is anybody knows better than to attempt to sound as if they know what they are actually talking about. So the job is hired out to someone else, mostly people who know even less. Movie stars call them publicists. Politicians call them communications specialists. Journalists call them flacks or hacks, use them and abuse them, and begrudgingly quote them. After a while on the job, the spokespeople become the only ones who actually *do* know anything.

Wayne LaPierre, the ethically challenged head of the National Rifle Association, who has belligerently championed gun rights in the United States for decades, found himself lamenting his notoriety in later years despite a hefty salary of almost $1 million a year from the non-profit—and bonuses bringing his income up to more than $5 million in 2015 alone. Facing a civil lawsuit filed by the New York attorney general about his high living and self-dealing in 2019, LaPierre was asked why he accepted free yacht trips in the Bahamas from an NRA contractor. His answer? The boat was a "security retreat." He recalled thinking, while he was on board, "Thank God I'm safe; nobody can get me here."

When questioned during a deposition about expenses totalling $300,000 for business suits, he complained about the trials of being a public figure: "I hardly ever—I don't really put on a suit except when I have to for NRA work. I get so harassed. The minute I put on a suit, I get I.D.'ed and somebody starts yelling at me. So to tell you the honest truth, I'm walking around most of the time—almost all the time in jeans and sunglasses and a ball cap because I am sick and my family is sick and tired of being yelled at, shouted at, screamed at, harassed, swatted, hacked, and generally abused."

People who come from old money are much like bankers. They know being rich is better than being famous, and they know being famous rarely ends well. They figured this out generations ago. They listened as their grandmothers and grandfathers told of the pitfalls of publicity. And frankly, other than being rich, most have done nothing to warrant fame anyway, rendering the entire matter moot.

So they situate their houses down long driveways behind lush vegetation, beyond the prying eyes of the public. They drive inconspicuous cars and avoid flashy clothes. If they must have wild parties, they are held on yachts where poor people and journalists can't intrude, or on estates with security. They don't talk to the media, and they never, ever air their dirty laundry in public...until, well, they do.

Despite all the training, all the warnings from relatives, all the signs the media is looking for only the slightest crack in the veneer, there's always an errant relative who allows the public a peek through the cracks in the facade of family unity. Sooner or later, every family has a spat, the spat escalates to legal action, and it all ends up in court, where lawyers circle like sharks for part of the fortune and journalists dig in for their fill of public documents (see Reason No. 6). And given that rich family problems are somehow far more compelling (if no less tawdry) than poor family problems, it's often a feast. Inevitably, rich families find themselves on front pages and homepages, in the crosshairs of the paparazzi and facing the wrath of the public. Ironically, what's at issue is usually the money and the power they already possess so much of—just not as much as they'd like.

Such was the case with the Haft family, which disintegrated in the mid-1990s during a struggle over who would run the family-owned retailing giant Dart Group Corp. It had been the picture of family harmony—until it wasn't. The feud pitted the mother, Gloria, and No. 1 son Robert against the father, Herbert, and No. 2 son Ronald in a series of lawsuits, countersuits and trials that lined the pockets of a legion of lawyers, decimated the family coffers and produced an endless stream of backstabbing scuttlebutt.

While the company crumbled, the elder Haft's wife accused him of having affairs and he accused her of taking a swing at him. Herbert accused his son Robert of not "paying attention to the business." Robert said, "My father wanted to be me, because people loved me. I was everything he wasn't. I feel sad for my father. He's taken tremendous action against the family and he still seems enraged."

Not long after the suit was settled with his brother and mother, the No. 2 son went after the father he was formerly allied with. Years later, Robert would recall the mess: "Let me tell you, I get calls all the time from people who say 'My father did this or my brother did that to me.' I always tell them the same thing: 'Go back and try to work it out.'"

That is not always possible. In 2007, billionaire Marilyn Carlson Nelson was sued by her drug-addicted son, Curtis Carlson Nelson, after he was removed from his position as president of Carlson Companies, the travel conglomerate her father founded. "Curtis used his company computer and company e-mail system—in 2006, while he was president and COO—to make purchases of large quantities of controlled substances from multiple on-line pharmacies," the company responded. "He also ordered a product called 'Quick-Detox,' which is advertised as helping users to 'pass any drug test!!!'"

Billionaire US media magnate Sumner Redstone, the late power-hungry boss of entertainment and media giant Viacom, was as famous for his family feuds as he was for the companies he ran. He faced his brother Edward's lawyers early in his career and publicly battled his daughter, Shari, for years over who would inherit control of the company. In 2006, he was sued by his son, Brent, and later that year by his nephew, Michael. "The two days that Brent and Michael sued me are two of the saddest days of my entire life," he said.

In 2016, his granddaughter Keryn joined others in a suit against him. The whole mess played out for decades on the front pages of newspapers. *Forbes* magazine, in a description that could apply to many old-money families, summed it up as "a Shakespearean tragedy, involving unhappy childhoods, bitter accusations by Sumner's son and nephew that he cheated them out of their inheritances, and, on the periphery, untimely deaths, mental illness and drug abuse."

Finally, a growing hallmark of the twenty-first century is the growth of an entirely new class of people: the utterly shameless. These people will stop at nothing in their quest for relevance. They revel in fame and all its consequences. For them, any publicity is good publicity. Reality TV stars such as the Kardashians, for example, seem immune to embarrassment over bad relationships, family bickering or questionable plastic surgeries. They are so desperate for attention, so hungry for the perceived benefits celebrity bestows, they don't seem to care about, or perhaps even notice, the downsides. All that attention, good and bad, has become somehow addictive, and they'll do anything for more, regardless of whether it is flattering or not.

Some politicians fall into this category. Unlike the Kardashians, they can't possibly be in it for the money, and while some may indeed be committed to public service, most are surely motivated by the idea of simply remaining in the public eye. Despite all the misery and mayhem of his presidency, for example, Donald Trump couldn't bear to give it up. Trump was obviously in love with his public image long before he got a taste of presidential power. He was secretly enthusiastic about sharing details of his failed marriages (if not necessarily his failed businesses) with the public. And he loved life as a kitschy pitchman and reality TV star. But it was being the centre of attention, good or bad, that was clearly the drug on which he was hooked. No insult could ever go unanswered. No opportunity to embarrass himself could ever be passed up.

Many others have done likewise, paving the way for Trump decades ago or following suit in recent times. And there may be no better example (among many) than Trump's personal lawyer, the former New York mayor Rudy Giuliani. Christened "America's Mayor" after September 11, 2001, he seemed addicted to the attention, revelling in the adoration, desperate for even more and painfully bereft after the public moved on to someone else. By 2020, acting as a lawyer for Trump's efforts to stay in power, Giuliani presented himself as a sad case indeed. Andrew Kirtzman, a biographer of Giuliani, wrote that his erratic behaviour in the dying days of the Trump presidency grew out of an "almost primal need to remain relevant."

The Butler Won't Do It

"It wasn't a tantrum as such but as reality goes, it was pretty far off the chart."
—Elton John, who once asked hotel staff if they could fix the weather

Reason No. 2 is it's hard for rich people to find good help.

It's not a cliché for nothing. A lot of superrich people can do only one thing well, whether it's athletics or business or art, and they spend so much time perfecting that one skill that they have very little time for anything else. Or perhaps they're workaholics, or just idle, and consider cooking, cleaning, gardening and pool maintenance beneath them. Whatever the reason, they need help with the more mundane chores the rest of us soldier through by rote. They need servants.

The merely affluent could be forgiven for believing it's not much of a challenge. And the simply well-off may wonder what all the fuss is about. After all, without the benefit of experience, we are left with the images created for us by writers. Fictional staff often seem as problem-free as mythical places such as Utopia, Shangri-La or Camelot. Jeeves, the famous manservant in stories by English author P.G. Wodehouse, appeared indispensable. And

Bruce Wayne, when he wasn't Batman, seemed virtually helpless without his loyal butler, Alfred. Early Hollywood television writers picked up the baton with creations such as Hazel, Hop Sing or Benson, or myriad characters who convinced poor viewers in network television's heyday that having help in the house was heartwarming and fun.

But the ultrarich know better, if only because they need so much more help. Hazel might be the perfect solution for the happily affluent family living in a modest home in the suburbs. But those who have a sprawling two-floor condominium in a big city are going to need a little (or probably a lot) more. A cook and cleaner, to be sure. A dog-walker perhaps. A driver maybe. In his book *Richistan*, Robert Frank recounts a conversation with Tim Blixseth, a lumber baron and philanthropist who, years later, would find himself in jail with financial problems. Long before his various misfortunes, Blixseth was telling Frank he had about sixty or seventy staff at his sprawling 240-acre estate near Palm Springs, California, when he was corrected by his wife, who said the number was actually 105. Replied Blixseth: "If it's 105 we have a problem."

Finding such assistants in the first place is a challenge; keeping them is a full-time job. To begin with, rich people need help in expensive neighbourhoods where gentrification has pushed poor people farther afield, making commuting more lengthy.

That's just the start. The superrich also need help at the summer place, not to mention the winter place. Such locations are also usually in rich enclaves where poor people, or even moderately rich people, cannot afford to live, if they are even allowed in. Ski resorts such as Whistler, British Columbia; Aspen, Colorado; or Gstaad, Switzerland, have rents tailored to the wealthy, grocery stores for gourmet chefs and shops with stuff folks want but don't need. Poor people can't afford any of it. Vacation centres such as

Muskoka, Ontario; the Hamptons, New York; and Palm Springs, California, all feature architectural masterpieces and sprawling status symbols, but not affordable housing.

More and more, vacation communities for the superrich are carved out of the pristine wilderness miles from nowhere. The new airport may be convenient for owners and guests arriving by private jet, but those able to cut the grass or clean the pool, do the dishes and make the beds will face a long drive on often treacherous roads in unpredictable weather conditions. The tendency for rich people to isolate themselves from everyone else has consequences many don't always appreciate, and when they are reminded of yawning income gaps by struggling employees, it can be anxiety-producing (see Reason No. 8).

Once, when they thought brutal exploitation was their birthright, it was easier for rich people. The history of civilization is the history of slaves, serfs, vassals and indentured servitude. Slaves pervaded ancient Mesopotamia. They may not have built the pyramids, but slavery existed in ancient Egypt, Greece and China. There were slaves in England before the Roman occupation, and for centuries after. Slavery helped build the British Empire. Slaves helped make America an economic powerhouse.

Where slavery was finally outlawed, unfree servitude persisted. Peasants in the early centuries of the second millennium were beholden to nobles and had no freedom. They had to work their land *and* their lord's land. They had to pay taxes to him. And they had no real freedom. Rich people, meanwhile, didn't care about fairness or whether people thought they were good employers or whether they paid anyone (see Reason No. 7). They didn't worry about unions or human rights. There was always another poor person to replace a servant who died of overwork or simply got fed up.

Only a century ago, even moderately rich people had servants for everyday tasks. Even servants had servants. There was just too much work. The richer you were, the more helpless—and more demanding—you became. In many cases, gentlemen of a certain social rank and income were not expected to do much at all, and even those with important jobs could not take on even simple tasks by themselves. The great and mighty Winston Churchill, for example, was incapable of dressing himself without help from his valet, John Gibson, who recalled, "He was social gentry...He sat there like a dummy and you dressed him." It's difficult to know if the man often called one of the most important leaders of the twentieth century considered that a problem, but most of the rest of us might.

And if dressing was difficult for some, imagine what it took to run an entire household. Those big English country homes were built to accommodate not just grand ballrooms but dank quarters down back staircases, from which legions of servants could be summoned with the ring of a bell. They were seen as little as possible and heard even less.

How would the fictional Downton Abbey, for example, have functioned without footmen, valets, housekeepers, chauffeurs, cooks, kitchen maids, scullery maids and stillroom maids, to name only a few? All those grand country manors of the past would have quicky been abandoned and crumbled to dust without help, and many of them did just that once the servants decamped for a better life. The problem of keeping the places staffed, let alone with the right people, became an ongoing challenge for the rich. The waxing and waning "servant problem" has been constant.

During the first decade of the twentieth century in Britain, more people were employed in domestic service than anything else. Many went off to the First World War in 1914. The problem waned a little when the men came back from the battlefield, and certainly during the Great Depression, when some people worked simply for room and board. Then it waxed again during the Second

World War, when women could get better jobs riveting aircraft, making bombs or helping plan invasions.

After the war, the invention of modern conveniences made many servants redundant. Washing machines, electric dryers, dishwashers, vacuum cleaners and microwave ovens became must-have items in many households, and prepared foods made dinner easier, so even if men still refused to do anything useful, middle-class women could manage their households by themselves. Then, as more women joined the workforce, even moderately rich people paid nannies and housekeepers to take care of the children and do menial tasks, but they paid them under the table rather than actually employing them (see Reason No. 7).

Rich people, after all, want servants at their beck and call, 24/7, but many don't want to pay them accordingly. Illegal immigrants are often desperate for such work, and it is often the very people who complain about immigrants, refugees and border security who are happy to underpay them for tasks they are too rich to do themselves.

Today, the middle class may not need help in the same manner they once did, but many still have trouble finding a plumber. And the furnace repair guy talks too much. Or the roofer is unreliable. Those too are rich people's problems. The more money you have, however, the more problems you have. More than a century has gone by since servants were everywhere in Britain. Robotic vacuums have been invented and takeout food is pervasive, but rich people still seem to need a lot of help: nannies, publicists, nutritionists, pilots, gardeners, dog-walkers, bodyguards, personal trainers, yacht captains, social-media specialists and various others doing stuff the rest of us have to figure out for ourselves.

Unfortunately, trusting strangers to do the right thing is a crapshoot. There's always some minion who's screwing something up. Even if rich people don't know how to do anything, they know how they want everything done. And they get angry when work is not up to their own ridiculous standards. Managing all that help can be a nightmare, especially if you are accustomed to perfection.

In his younger days, Elton John had regular problems with the help. In a 1997 documentary, *Tantrums & Tiaras*, directed by his husband, David Furnish, John has a meltdown on camera about incompetent staff before a performance: "All this months of work that I've put in and someone leaves a fucking bag in a car. Fuck it... I'll do everything my fucking self in future."

Alas, even he could never live up to his standards, let alone force them on the hapless servants. He once famously complained to hotel management about the weather outside his suite. "I'd been up for a couple of days at the Inn on the Park, as it was then, on Park Lane in London, and I was still up at 11 o'clock in the morning. And I rang the office and spoke to a guy called Robert Keown and I said, 'Robert, it's far too windy here, can you do something about it,'" recalled John years later. "It wasn't a tantrum as such but as reality goes, it was pretty far off the chart." In 2021, he reflected on his years of bad behaviour toward others: "I'm not proud of that stuff, no, it makes me shudder. My behaviour was so erratic and so unpredictable. And it's still in me, to explode at any moment."

Poor people can be just as erratic; the rest of us simply don't hear about it. And so that kind of conduct become endless fodder for the tabloids and social media (see Reason No. 1). The queen in this department may be supermodel Naomi Campbell, who was accused of assault over the better part of a decade by various aides and helpers and was convicted four times.

In 2000, she pleaded guilty to assaulting her personal assistant with a phone. In 2006, she was arrested for assaulting her drug counsellor. In 2007, she pleaded guilty to physically abusing her former housekeeper. In 2008, she kicked one police officer called to remove her from a plane and spat on another. That came after an obscenity-filled tirade to the captain and crew about a missing suit-case. In 2010, she was in the news again after her driver said she assaulted him. "If I'm gonna be remembered for something," Camp-bell once told TV personality Barbara Walters, "I will be remembered for being a bitch, but a hard-working bitch. And a loyal bitch."

It wasn't anger or incompetence but apparently personal demons that caused strife between charismatic television cook Nigella Lawson and her staff in 2013. The self-proclaimed domestic goddess charged two sisters who acted as her personal assistants with fraud after they racked up hundreds of thousands of pounds on her husband's business credit cards during an ongoing shopping spree. But the Italian-born sisters, Francesca and Elisabetta Grillo, fought back in court, telling the jury that Lawson condoned the spending as long as they didn't tell her husband about her drug use.

The trial, and all its sordid details, played out for weeks in the media. Lawson admitted to taking drugs to deal with "intimate terrorism" by her husband, the reclusive art collector and adver-tising executive Charles Saatchi. Ultimately, the jury found both sisters not guilty in 2013. After it was over, the sisters spoke to the media: "It's mortifying for her, it's mortifying for us, it's mortifying for everybody involved," said Francesca. The following year, after the trial—and her marriage—was over, Lawson herself reflected on the situation: "I've had better times."

Often, such embarrassing details emerge even without a court case. A few helpers, no matter how seemingly discreet or loyal, are ready for a chat with the media sooner or later. It often comes at the end of one's employment, and as that is inevitable, the only reason there aren't more tell-alls filling the newspapers and lining the shelves of bookstores is the ubiquitous presence of non-disclosure agreements. Given that some celebrities ask even dates or hookups to sign to them, it's basically a given that few servants are hired without them.

Still, some stories can't be contained. In 2016, Kanye West and Kim Kardashian felt the wrath of a bodyguard, Steve Stanulis, a former Chippendales dancer and police officer, who found himself no longer in their employ after only fifteen days. Stanulis said he was fired for talking to Kim by a jealous West. Calling the rapper "self-absorbed," Stanulis recommended West "chill the fuck out." Kardashian was later sued in Los Angeles County Superior Court by seven workers who said she did not pay them for hours worked and did not give them meal and rest breaks or pay stubs.

Some employees don't require a courtroom to spill the beans, but the threat of court action sometimes helps smooth things over. Compact singing sensation Justin Bieber was sued by his beefy bodyguard, former Israeli soldier Moshe Benabou, who alleged he was somehow injured when Bieber punched him during a tirade in 2012. They settled out of court. Bieber was also charged with assault in 2014 for punching his chauffeur.

Britney Spears's former bodyguard, Fernando Flores, sued her for sexual harassment in 2010. The suit alleged that "commencing at or about the time of the Plaintiff's employment, Defendant Britney Spears made repeated and unwanted sexual advances to Plaintiff, summoning Plaintiff to her room at her residence for no other purpose or reason than to expose her naked or near naked body to Plaintiff." The bodyguard settled out of court.

In 1999, action star Sylvester Stallone was sued by five former cooks and cleaners after they were fired six days into a fifteen-day contract. They claimed they underwent daily searches for possible thefts, and that Stallone expected maids to check guests' suitcases "to see if they took towels or silverware" when leaving. Other decrees included not making eye contact with the star and not speaking to Stallone's mother, "nor will you let her talk to you," they alleged.

Sometimes spilling the beans can be disguised in a bestselling novel. Fashion queen Anna Wintour, famous as editor of *Vogue* magazine, was clearly unimpressed when a former assistant, Lauren Weisberger, wrote *The Devil Wears Prada* in 2003. The book featured a tyrannical fashion editor who terrorizes her staff. It is widely considered an inside view of the so-called grand dame of fashion.

When the book was made into a successful movie of the same name in 2006 starring Meryl Streep, it wasn't just the fashion world and the bookworms who drew parallels but now the entire movie-going public. Streep's character was distant and aloof and treated the help with disdain, forcing them to run impossible personal errands and ordering them about 24/7.

Non-fiction accounts of Wintour confirmed this unflattering reputation, now widespread. Wintour, who was known for ignoring anyone who wasn't rich and famous, had become one of them. In his book on Wintour, *Front Row*, Jerry Oppenheimer wrote that "while Anna was sleek and chic, she was harshly critical and sarcastic, and spiritedly made fun of people who weren't."

Even more terrifying for rich (and famous) people are the likes of Chuck Jones, a former publicist for Marla Maples, the second trophy wife of Donald Trump. After years of managing the media storm around Maples, Jones caused problems of his own by stealing more than seventy pairs of her shoes, with which he later admitted to having a "sexual relationship." His foot fetish was caught on hidden security cameras (he was filmed licking some of them) after Maples noticed her collection was shrinking rather than growing.

Long before Jones's illicit affair with Maples's shoes became public, he had been her biggest booster. "The media has portrayed Marla as a disorganized, shapely bimbo, and that is not what she is," he told *Vanity Fair* in 1990. "I wouldn't let anything happen to her. Her friendship is the biggest present I have." And Maples later told an interviewer how important he had been to her: "Chuck was someone I trusted."

After the conviction, Maples was less enthusiastic, and released a statement: "I hope that in the future Mr. Jones will seek the guidance I believe he needs." Clearly, Jones did not get that guidance, or enough of it, as he was back in the news more than a decade later, sentenced to a jail term for stalking Maples, by then Trump's ex-wife and sometimes described, like Trump's first wife, as a socialite.

Less scary for rich people, perhaps, but sometimes no less mortifying, are personal assistants, nannies and other household minions who get even closer to some members of the family. There are many untold stories over millennia of aging men lusting after the younger help, but in an age of tabloids and social media, much of it has become a seamy matter of public record. In 2011, the world would learn the sordid details of how iconic muscleman and former California governor Arnold Schwarzenegger fathered a child with his family's housekeeper while his wife was pregnant, and kept it secret for more than ten years. In an interview on Reddit in 2014, Schwarzenegger was asked, "Of all the things that you are famous for...which are you least proud of?" His answer: "I'm least proud of the mistakes I made that caused my family pain and split us up."

Schwarzenegger's dalliance was particularly infamous, but he wasn't alone. Actor Jude Law's engagement to Sienna Miller ended when his relationship with their twenty-six-year-old nanny became public, and the media descended like vultures to an unclaimed carcass. Singer Gwen Stefani divorced husband Gavin Rossdale for the same reason, according to *Us Weekly*. Mick Jagger allegedly had sex with his nanny on the kitchen counter while his wife, Jerry Hall, was asleep in another room, according to Claire Houseman, who recounted the incident to a biographer. Supermodel Christie Brinkley divorced her forty-nine-year-old husband, Peter Cook, after a sordid trial that aired a lot of dirty family laundry, including his affair with his eighteen-year-old assistant. Ethan Hawke married his nanny after his breakup with Uma Thurman. And Robin Williams left his first wife for the couple's nanny. Geena Davis left her husband, director Renny Harlin, the day her personal assistant, Tiffany Bowne, gave birth to his child. This is the kind of thing the tabloids gobble up (see Reason No. 1).

Yes, it can be lonely being rich, even more so being famous. Rich people have trouble relating to poor people, and poor people can't really relate to rich people. And celebrities can't really hang out with fans, adoring, unruly or otherwise. That's why the rich and famous stick together. Still, it has to end sooner or later. Their friends go home, and they're left alone with the help. Professional liaisons are often inevitable, even with poor working people, but for the rich, such matters are often more complicated, and more public. German supermodel Heidi Klum dated her bodyguard after she divorced the British singer-songwriter Seal. Amy Winehouse did likewise with her bodyguard after she got a divorce. Princess Stephanie of Monaco married her bodyguard. Pamela Anderson's fifth husband was formerly her bodyguard, as was Elizabeth Taylor's eighth. Hilary Duff dated her personal trainer.

Brian Wilson of the Beach Boys was so enthralled with micromanaging therapist Eugene Landy that he promoted him to manager, then music collaborator, producer and financial partner before issuing a restraining order against him.

Poor people have such liaisons too, of course, but since they have fewer staff, they have fewer options. Chauffeurs, hairdressers, backup singers, cooks and cleaners—many start out as employees, matriculate to friends and finally graduate as lovers—or ex-lovers.

And then there is the phenomenon of the celebrity entourage, where the lines between friend, family and employee are blurred. While some servants are expected to be neither seen nor heard, others are front and centre—travelling in a posse, running interference in airports, bullying fans or just picking up coffee, they remain at the ready for the boss 24/7. Elvis Presley had a famous entourage dubbed the Memphis Mafia by the media, filled with family, friends and flunkies. Drake, Diddy and Rihanna are known for their crews.

In his heyday as an NBA star, Allen Iverson often travelled with an entourage reported to be in the neighbourhood of fifty people, an astounding number even in a profession where large entourages are common, and a financial burden to boot, even for someone who earned $200 million playing basketball. In his biography of Iverson, *Not a Game*, Kent Babb writes that Iverson "rarely drove his own cars, and there was a network of sycophants and coattail riders who were happy to do all manner of tasks." But Iverson described many of the activities as simply "laughing and joking and playing cards and doing the things that we do."

The entourage, then, is a full-service operation: it offers rich (and famous) people not just help but company, friendship and therapy. Alas, such therapy can be expensive. Iverson was known to be generous, gifting cars, jewelry and houses to friends and relatives, but he was a gambler and an overshopper, who was apparently reluctant to pay his bills. In 2012, a jeweller sued him for unpaid bills and a judge eventually ordered him to cough up $850,000. By that time, the crew had decamped, and Iverson found himself without the company he cherished.

Everybody needs a friend; rich people seem to have trouble finding enough. And only a few people truly like to be alone. But for influential pop artist Andy Warhol, the entourage was an artistic endeavour and business venture. Friends, acquaintances and hangers-on offered amusement and inspiration as well as labour. "He didn't talk, Andy," recalled writer Fran Lebowitz. "What he wanted to do was get you to talk. He was a vampire. He wanted to take things from people."

Warhol collected dozens of associates over the years, acting both as discreet observer and ringleader of a carnival of artists, musicians, wannabe actors, drug users and the sons and daughters of rich people. Many were not so much socialites, groupies or posse members as what Warhol labelled "superstars." They appeared in his films and accompanied him on social outings, inspired his art and kept him company, a revolving door of "it" people who were famous for fifteen minutes, a prophetic phrase coined by Warhol himself. Mary Woronov, a painter, writer and actor who appeared in one of Warhol's films, said it was "like a medieval court of lunatics. You pledged allegiance to the king—King Warhol. Yet oddly there was no hierarchy."

The richer rich people get, the less they seem to be able to accomplish without help. In due course, their staffs grow in accordance with their salaries. As the entourage gets bigger, friends and employees become indistinguishable, and interchangeable. As in most groups that spend too much time together, discord inevitably bubbles and brews—and finally erupts into a hot media mess.

Finally, while personal assistants, trainers, publicists and pilots can be troublesome for rich people, there may be no helper more problematic than the money guys: personal business managers, investment gurus and financial advisors. While most of us worry about making money, rich people worry about keeping it. It's stressful, it's complicated and it's risky. Like the rest of us, they haven't a clue how it should be done, nor are they much interested in anything more than the bottom line.

Clearly, many are not as particular about money management as they are about such things as shoes, drugs and how to arrange the pillows on the poolside chaise longue, if the number of lawsuits between rich people and their financial advisers is any indication. They discover too late they should have been watching the piggy bank a little closer.

Embattled movie star Johnny Depp went after the Management Group and two of its attorneys for $25 million in 2017, saying they took money they didn't earn and failed to pay his taxes, an oversight that cost him more than $5 million in penalties. They countersued, alleging the actor lived an "ultra-extravagant lifestyle that often knowingly cost Depp in excess of $2 million per month to maintain, which he simply could not afford."

Overspending actor Nicolas Cage had a similar problem, accusing his business manager Samuel J. Levin of negligence. But Levin said Cage ignored his warning that he couldn't afford his $30-million-a-year spending habit, and instead insisted on buying "15 personal residences" plus a "flotilla of yachts" and a "squadron of Rolls-Royces," among many other indulgences.

"Piano Man" Billy Joel once sued his manager for $90 million and was awarded $2 million. Actor Uma Thurman sued a wayward manager, and pop star Rihanna sued her accountants.

Despite all those troubles, however, the help that may cost rich people the most and create the biggest problems are the investment operators. Most are hard-working, well-informed, trustworthy and morally upright. But history is peppered with those who are not. Conniving money managers, thieving chief executives and fraudulent business leaders have been preying on the rich for centuries, living fantastically extravagant lifestyles to maintain the illusion of wealth, siphoning money from their hapless victims while mingling socially with them. It inevitably ends poorly for everyone involved, but that doesn't seem to stop history from repeating itself, mostly because rich people want to get richer (see Reason No. 5).

In 2010, Scott W. Rothstein, a high-flying Florida lawyer, was sentenced to fifty years in a federal prison after running a $1.2-billion Ponzi scheme. That same year, Tom Petters, a Minnesota business owner, also received a fifty-year prison sentence for an unrelated scheme that cost investors $3.7 billion. Only two years later, in 2012, R. Allen Stanford, a real estate speculator and business owner, was sentenced to 110 years in prison for a $7-billion scheme.

None of them, nor their ilk, nor indeed most of those who invested with them, seem to have learned much from the fate of history's most scandalous swindler (besides Charles Ponzi himself)—Bernard Madoff, who took hundreds of individuals and institutions for billions and was sentenced to 150 years in prison, where he has since died. Kevin Bacon—who, with his wife, Kyra Sedgwick, was among those who found themselves out of luck and out of pocket when the scheme crumbled—likely understated the sentiments of many: "It was a bad day."

The Spite Fence

"The absurdity would be laughable even to me if I wasn't a direct participant."
—Bill Gross, a billionaire entangled in an escalating dispute with his neighbour

Reason No. 3 is that rich people have problems with other rich people.

Many of us have problems with our neighbours. There's often someone next door or down the way who's making noise, storing rusty vehicles in the driveway or endlessly smoking meat on the backyard barbecue. And property-line issues seem constant no matter where you live, as any local politician will attest. These issues, though, always seem bigger, more deeply entrenched and endlessly interesting when rich people are involved, often because they can afford to employ lawyers and engage the court system, thereby providing the public with a buffet of public documents upon which to feast (see Reason No. 1).

While modestly prosperous people are obliged to live in old houses and can barely afford minor repairs, the ultrarich seem forever bent on improving their mansions, tearing down inadequate residences and indulging in ever grander construction projects on their properties. As a consequence, they make a bigger audio and visual racket, upsetting the orderly flow of things and changing gracious neighbourhoods. And nobody, rich or poor, likes change, unless they themselves are responsible for it.

As well, as rich people's neighbours are also usually rich people themselves, their voices are louder, their issues bigger, their lawyers more numerous. No house is too big or too much for a rich person, unless it's the rich person's house next door or down the street, in which case it is always too big and too much. Big houses always seem to lead to big problems.

That is how the case of a house built by the late TV schlock king Aaron Spelling, who created programs such as *Dynasty, Charlie's Angels* and *The Love Boat,* came to find its way into the newspapers in the 1980s. Just as a new generation of indulgent ultrashoppers were taxiing for takeoff, Spelling bought the former estate of crooning movie star Bing Crosby, just down the street from the notorious Playboy Mansion in Los Angeles. He immediately tore it down for something a little grander: a 56,000-square-foot building with 123 rooms he christened "The Manor." The rich neighbours were incensed by the endless construction, grumbled that it spoiled their view, and complained it was just too big. One nearby resident complained to the *Los Angeles Times* that the house employed "look-at-me-I'm-rich" architecture, while another said he was "not excited about the visibility of this wealth." These complainers chose to ignore the fact that most were themselves living in mansions on vast properties in one of the wealthiest neighbourhoods in Los Angeles, indeed the world.

Decades later, such battles remain alive and well. Legendary footballer David Beckham and his former Spice Girl wife, Victoria, often seem mired in such contretemps. In 2014, the couple angered a neighbour with plans for a £12-million renovation to their £31-million home in West London, dubbed "Beckingham Palace II" ("Beckingham Palace" had previously been in the news) by the

British tabloids. Plans included adding air-conditioning, a wine cellar and another bedroom. The neighbour said it would affect drainage, appearance, structural stability and the historic aspects of the building.

But five years later, it was the Beckhams themselves who were complaining, saying they would lose their privacy if renovations at the pile next door were permitted. Not two months after that, they were again the targets of vitriol from different neighbours, this time at their country home in West Oxfordshire. Residents were already annoyed by the Beckhams' conversion of a traditional farmhouse into a luxury dwelling complete with a guard house, but their plan to dig a 28,000-square-foot ornamental lake was the living end, apparently. The plans were described as both "ugly" and "monstrous."

That description may not have sufficed for outraged neighbours in nearby Kensington after a homeowner there painted her mansion in white and red stripes, spurred by a neighbourhood tiff. It all started when Zipporah Lisle-Mainwaring, a property developer, had big plans for the house she bought in 2012 for £15 million in posh Kensington. She wanted to demolish the place and build a new structure with a two-storey "iceberg" super-basement, an amenity increasingly common in rich downtown neighbourhoods with height restrictions, but one involving a great deal of dump trucks and construction noise. Neighbours objected to the project, which would have accommodated a gym, cinema and pool on the lower floors, and the local council squelched it in 2015.

In alleged retaliation, Lisle-Mainwaring decorated the house in the offending barber-shop motif. "It's very fluorescent and very garish," said a neighbour. "Without sounding very pretentious, it isn't very Kensington. It's more Camden or something like that." The local council agreed, and with support from the outraged neighbours, immediately ordered the place repainted in plain white. "It rather supports the impression people have had that she is not very neighbourly and neither does it do her case much good," said local councillor Timothy Coleridge.

Alas, the lady was not for turning. Lisle-Mainwaring took the candy stripes to the nation's highest court, which supported her. Today, miraculously, a new structure (without stripes) stands on the site, and the neighbourhood squabble is history, as is the off-beat tourist attraction the affair spawned.

Sometimes it's not incongruity with the neighbourhood that is the problem, but the exact opposite. In 2014, a house being built in the swanky Toronto neighbourhood of Forest Hill found its way into the courts (and headlines) when a nearby couple noticed it looked suspiciously like their own eight-thousand-square-foot architectural wonder. "When we saw tradespeople unrelated to the construction of our home standing on our driveway taking photographs, which they said were to better copy details for the house they were building, we were very disappointed," said Jason and Jodi Chapnik in a letter to the editor of the *Toronto Star*. "We watched the other house go up and the similarities build."

Architects (and the law) frown on such rip-offs, and rich homeowners are rarely impressed with the idea of seeing copycat buildings in the vicinity after they've spent so much to make theirs unique. After the dispute hit the news, the Chapniks were the targets of unsympathetic commentary from bystanders who didn't fully grasp the intricacies of architectural copyright.

As often as not, it is aesthetics as much as renovation noise and construction dust that annoys rich people, and as they like to control everything about their environments, they are particularly sensitive to it. In 2009, neighbours in a rural area near Seattle were appalled when new homeowners painted their building bright purple. Not only had the arresting colour "polluted our views," as one homeowner described it, the ugly building also had neighbouring homeowners worried about their property values. They asked for a tax break from the municipality because of it.

The simmering feud escalated when one neighbour took to an adjacent field with his lawnmower and carved a sprawling message into the sod. A grass-cutting project so large it could be seen on Google Earth (and subsequently printed in various newspapers), it read simply "A HOLE," and included an arrow pointing at the new building.

This kind of nasty back-and-forth between neighbours is sometimes discussed in property and nuisance law as a "spite fence," a "spite wall" or even a "spite house"—often defined legally as any kind of division that is intended to annoy the people next door. There are endless examples, but most have one thing in common: the perpetrators generally have too much time and money. The most famous architect of such a structure may be Charles Crocker, a rich railroad tycoon who wanted to buy his neighbour's house in San Francisco in the 1800s. When the neighbour, Nicholas Yung, refused to sell, Crocker built a forty-foot fence around three sides of Yung's house. It would stand for years before Yung died, the property finally sold, and the wall was removed. Spite walls were subsequently outlawed and Crocker's sprawling mansion was destroyed in the 1906 San Francisco earthquake.

In 2022, after his neighbours called municipal bylaw officers about a dead tree on the property line, a moderately rich homeowner in Burlington, a community near Toronto, came up with a particularly creative equivalent of the spite fence. After he was forced to pay a removal fee for the dead tree, he built a raccoon house in his backyard, decorated in colourful dildos and in full view of the neighbours' deck. The dispute found its way into the local media, and into a monologue on *Jimmy Kimmel Live!* a few days later.

In 2013, a publicity-hungry Detroit strip-club owner erected a twelve-foot-high sculpture of "a middle finger salute" in the backyard of a home he had only recently purchased. When local media came calling, Alan Markovitz said the sculpture was aimed at the neighbour next door, who he claimed had had an affair with his wife, now his ex-wife. The installation, he said, cost $7,000 and lit up every night. "I'm so over her," he said of his wife. Her alleged lover? Apparently not so much.

Similarly, it was an art installation that apparently began a years-long dispute between neighbours in Laguna Beach. Billionaire bond investor Bill Gross installed a $1-million, twenty-two-foot-long blown glass sculpture by acclaimed artist Dale Chihuly in the yard next to his oceanside mansion. At some point after that, Gross added a protective netting around it. His neighbour, Mark Towfiq, a tech entrepreneur, took offence to the white netting, saying it spoiled his view of the azure ocean, and lodged a complaint with the municipality. According to Towfiq, Gross retaliated by playing loud music, rap songs and the theme to *Gilligan's Island*, on an endless loop into the night. The case ended up in the courts in 2020, and in news reports across the country. Said Gross: "The absurdity would be laughable even to me if I wasn't a direct participant."

Sometimes rich people are annoyed by neighbours who aren't even in residence. This is the case for rich neighbours of Johnny Depp, the owner of a castle in West Hollywood that he rarely uses. Not only did he buy the neighbouring houses for various uses, including a personal studio, he surrounded the place with enough vegetation to completely obscure it from the street.

But it hasn't stopped gawking tourists from making the pilgrimage daily. "We were getting these vans with open tops and the people are talking, and cheering and yelling, and it's been annoying," said John Ryan, a resident on the street for almost three decades, in an interview with the *New York Post*. According to the *Post*, Ryan had earlier taken to TripAdvisor.com, begging tourists to stay away: "As a neighbour of Mr. Depp, I implore you to please not go there! All you're doing is bothering everyone in the area with no pay-off! I have lived across the street since Mr. Depp moved in many years ago, and I have seen him ONE TIME. Trust me, you won't see him, his house, his kids, his wife, his dogs."

Even when they are wealthy enough to isolate themselves completely, rich people seem to upset the folks next door. Mark Zuckerberg had already left a battlefield of annoyed neighbours around his San Francisco compound when he moved on to Hawaii in 2014, paying more than $100 million for 750 acres on the coast of Kauai. Unfortunately for his new neighbours, Zuckerberg felt the place required a rock wall to reduce road noise in the semi-rural area. Rich neighbours, who had sued the previous owner for earlier attempts to ensure privacy, were unimpressed, saying it reduced sea breezes and obstructed their views. Several purchases later, when Zuckerberg and his wife had amassed more than 1,400 acres, the problems continued. Lawyers filed "quiet title" suits, saying Zuckerberg stomped on the rights of local Hawaiians who may own bits and pieces of land within the estate. Kapua Sproat, a law professor at the University of Hawaii, summed up the mess in an interview with the *Guardian*: "This is the face of neocolonialism."

Half an ocean away, in Marin County, California, *Star Wars* filmmaker George Lucas had plans to expand the famed studio on his secluded 6,100-acre property. For decades, he had operated there without incident, developing his production company on what would become Skywalker Ranch, as he called it, in one of the wealthiest areas in the United States. But plans to expand in 2009 irked some of the rich locals, saying the project would "dwarf the average Costco warehouse" and threaten the ecology of the valley.

The skirmish simmered until 2012, when Lucas's company finally pulled the plug on it, saying he did not have support from enough area residents. Instead, he announced plans to finance an affordable housing project there, much to the chagrin, to say nothing of shock and outrage, of the rich locals who had opposed his original studio plan. Some observers remarked on the delicious irony the situation presented: rich, woke liberals who traditionally lobbied governments for more affordable housing were suddenly less enthusiastic about it coming to their exclusive neighbourhood. "It's inciting class warfare," said Carolyn Lenert, head of the neighbourhood organization. For his part, Lucas insisted his plans were made with the best philanthropic intentions and not out of spite: "I've been surprised to see some people characterize this as vindictive."

It's bad enough being rich and having other rich people upset your sensibilities, but it can be even worse if you are rich *and* famous and have *poor* interlopers wandering near your private Eden. That problem once faced pop star Madonna on her sprawling estate, Ashcombe House, in Wiltshire, England, which has laws giving the public the right of access to what is called "open country." That meant any old nobody could wander across parts of the 142 hectares that Madonna owned with her then husband, the director Guy Ritchie, and they just couldn't tolerate it. Their privacy was being invaded, their human rights infringed, the couple argued. They won a partial victory in the courts, which decided some—but not all—of the lands in question would be private. They weren't alone in their concerns. The government had changed the "right to roam" laws in England and expanded the "open country" areas that so-called ramblers could access on foot. Many landowners were worried not only about privacy, but also about property values, and the pop star's luxurious spread helped the issue gain traction in the media. Said Ben Thomas of the Country Landowners Association: "Imagine how pleased fans will be to hear they can walk around her estate."

The same challenge—keeping poor people at bay—faces superrich Americans, many of whom have bought up large swaths of untamed geography in places like Colorado, which are bisected by rivers that are frequented by the less affluent. These interlopers, troublesome anglers or river rafters, are under the impression that such waterways, but not the shorelines, are owned by the taxpayers. Rich landowners disagree and consider anyone in—or on—the water flowing through their land trespassers. The simmering battle —with environmentalists, landowners, outdoors advocates and lawyers lining up on all sides—pits the poor against the rich as populations multiply and a desire for wilderness experiences grows.

Other outdoor recreationalists in the United States, many of them hunters, are finding their last frontiers of public land boxed in by private property bought by superrich city folk disinclined to allow hunters to traverse it. As much as fifteen million acres of public land across the United States is surrounded by private property. In what has all the markings of class warfare, hunters and public land activists have creatively experimented with ways to access it, with help from GPS technology, but landowners are unimpressed. The battle, when and if it is finally decided, may come down to who owns property rights in the air rights *above* the ground.

Perhaps the biggest neighbourhood problem for rich people is their inability to leave a small footprint. At the height of his fifteen minutes of fame in the 1980s, the ferocious actor and wrestler known as Mr. T instituted a landscaping plan around his Chicago home that was less than calmly received by local residents. The once-famous actor had one hundred mature trees removed—some of them gleefully chopped down with a chainsaw by the owner himself—on an estate he bought in the city's Lake Forest neighbourhood, which happened to have been named for its foliage. "I was dumbfounded," said one neighbour. "I just could not believe somebody could be that destructive to something that took God maybe 60 years to grow. And they're gone. Just gone." Another lamented: "If Mr. T doesn't like trees, why didn't he build a house in the cornfields?"

But as rich people know by now, that probably wouldn't have worked either. It seems no location is too isolated, no property so private, that it doesn't catch the eye—and the ire—of rich neighbours. A casual observer might be inclined to believe a remote island, for example, would be a haven, a personal space where rich people can behave badly, play loud music and host wild keggers, but someone always seems to be watching, and they're usually other rich people.

Those who build sprawling cottages in peaceful rural areas or on quiet lakes are almost always in for some trouble from at least some of the locals. A few, usually the poorer, are often happy someone has finally arrived to fix up their neck of the woods, boost real estate values or hire locals to work on endless construction and maintenance projects, but rich neighbours can be another matter.

Back in the day, their own construction project may have dwarfed every other structure in the district, blasted the bedrock, destroyed countless trees and spoiled the view, but that was years ago, before things got out of hand. Now it's different. Wilderness is disappearing and the homes are getting too big and too numerous. What that really means is their houses are no longer the biggest and most impressive, and what was fine for them a decade ago is unacceptable today.

This is what happened in the Canadian cottaging community of Muskoka, an expensive vacation area north of Toronto, at the turn of the new millennium. That's when neighbourhood complaints about construction megaprojects began reaching a new crescendo: ever-bigger lakefront residences with sprawling boathouses and float-plane docks were apparently wrecking the place, disfiguring the forest, mutilating the shoreline and interrupting the alleged serenity, even though this process had been under way for the better part of a century. Cottage owners there have included Cindy Crawford and Kenny G. Once again, no cottage is ever too big unless it's the neighbour's cottage. "Seeing what these ignorant rich people are doing disgusts me to my soul," said one cottager in response to a petition launched by Roger Oatley, who objected in particular to a residence on Sugarloaf Island. Said Susan Eplett, vice president of the Muskoka Lakes Association: "People up here are having a real problem with the scale of development on residential and commercial properties."

I have friends who once spent their summers on a breathtakingly beautiful island in Georgian Bay, Ontario, and I was often lucky enough to be invited as a guest. Georgian Bay is not far from Muskoka, but cottage development is more sparse. From time to time, my host would note the presence of "neighbours." To which I would reply quizzically: "What neighbours?" To me, their island seemed isolated. I could see no other cottages from the beach or the dock save a single structure far, far across the water. Foreign boats rarely entered the bay unless they were visitors, no unwanted wakes ever rocked the dock or disturbed the serenity. The water was calm and clear, the only sound the whispering pines in a summer breeze.

But ignorance is bliss. Unlike me, my host was aware of what I couldn't see. There was, in fact, another cottage or two on the island, though the owners were never seen or heard, at least by me, and the buildings themselves were hidden from view. Still, for inhabitants, the island wasn't as secluded as it appeared to a mere visitor, even a regular one. We used to joke about the ever-present possibility of some kind of invasion from nearby lands. I realized then I had made the same mistake many rich people—and poor people, for that matter—make when moving to a new property: insufficient reconnaissance.

Every neighbourhood has its secrets, open or otherwise. It may be obvious that the guy next door has painted the garage door an ugly colour, or has bad taste in lawn art, but you can't know for sure if the other neighbour plays loud music around the clock, or whether they are poised to take unreasonable offence to how you shovel your walk or plant your garden.

Likewise, a rich person may be able to scope out the expansive dock at the cottage next door, even meet the owners for cocktails, but how can you know exactly how many boats they have, or how many more they are planning to buy, or how big they are, or how much wake they create, or how noisy the engines are, or how many teenagers they will have on weekends, or how often they go water-skiing, or tubing, or fishing, or just buzzing around on personal watercraft spoiling the view and the serenity, or whether they'll host loud kegger parties every weekend featuring expensive DJs or rock bands? In turn, how can they know what problems the new neighbours might introduce? No matter how amiable or distant, neighbours are still neighbours.

The late Scottish actor Sean Connery, famous for his iconic portrayal of James Bond, and his wife engaged in such a long-running legal battle with neighbours over noise and renovations at their New York condominium that a judge finally had enough. She told them both they must get the court's permission before any further legal action because they were not getting any closer to co-operating in the building's management. "Unfortunately, the litigation, as it has been conducted," said the judge, "is interfering with, not advancing that goal."

A judge presiding over a dispute involving the driveway between the Hollywood Hills home of actor Minnie Driver and her neighbour, Daniel Perlmutter, in 2018 seemed equally disappointed. "The jury is going to say, 'All these lawyers—they're making a federal case out of this,'" said Los Angeles Superior Court Judge Rita Miller. "The heart of this case is who's richer than who, I guess."

Leonardo DiCaprio irked his neighbours in the Hollywood

Hills when he allegedly wrecked their garden while building a basketball court adjacent to it. Dennis Rodman's neighbours in Newport Beach called the police more than eighty times, complaining mostly of loud parties and the comings and goings of a helicopter. In 1990, a Superior Court judge in Los Angeles County forced Madonna to trim a tree and hedges because they spoiled the view of her neighbour in the Hollywood Hills.

Actor Val Kilmer faced the wrath of his neighbours when he applied to turn his ranch near Santa Fe, New Mexico, into a bed and breakfast in 2010. The locals had no problem with the plans, but they were still angry about comments the *Top Gun* and *Tombstone* star had made years earlier about the people who lived near him. Among the hurtful accusations: 80 per cent "of the people in my county are drunk" and Vietnam veterans are "borderline criminal" and became soldiers because they "couldn't finagle a scholarship." Kilmer said he was misquoted, but the neighbours and the veterans wanted an apology before they would okay his development plans. The San Miguel County Commission invited the star to drop by and explain himself. Kilmer finally apologized—and got his permit.

Some of us might be inclined to believe being rich would make it easy to avoid such problems. After all, poor people are usually stuck with bad neighbours. They don't have enough money to sue them, and they can't afford to move. What's more, being working stiffs, many don't have the time or energy to indulge in ridiculous battles. So they endure. Rich people, on the other hand, have lots of money and time. And though they are able to move anywhere they want, they are used to getting their way, and they don't like losing. So they stick it out, dig in for the long fight, and can't really comprehend why small problems mushroom into big ones.

This was clearly the case with a feud between Peter Nygård, once a stinking-rich Canadian fashion executive, and his billionaire neighbour Louis Bacon, a New York hedge fund operator, in the exclusive enclave of Lyford Cay in the Bahamas. At first, Nygård, a flamboyant and creepy party animal allegedly fond of teenage girls who loved showing off his garish 150,000-square-foot estate, and Bacon, a subdued philanthropist who avoided the spotlight and focused on conservation pursuits, were amiable neighbours. But cracks began to appear in 2005 over a shared driveway and widened into a disagreement over noise in 2007, and by 2010 the point of contention was environmental damage caused by development.

Eventually, Nygård was charged with redistributing sand to expand his property, which he egotistically named Nygård Cay. When the Bahamian government ordered him to fix the mess, he blamed Bacon and a battle royale ensued. Nygård hired operatives to besmirch Bacon's name, helped finance fake news websites and organize anti-Bacon rallies aimed at associating him with various misdeeds, racist activities, even murder.

In turn, Bacon, who said he feared for his life, helped fund lawyers and others to investigate allegations that Nygård raped teenage girls in the Bahamas and fed information to media organizations. A series of lawsuits and countersuits ensued. "Their battle became a cottage industry for opportunists," wrote the *New York Times* in 2020.

Today, Nygård Cay is mostly abandoned and in disrepair, its owner in jail, and the company bankrupt. Nygård is charged with multiple counts of sexual assault, sex trafficking, racketeering and conspiracy and awaits extradition to the United States. Bacon, who tried to sell his property for $35 million at the height of the madness, dismantled his hedge fund to focus on a more restful life of family, philanthropy and conservation—and perhaps his half dozen or so other properties across the world, where one assumes his relations with the neighbours are less stressful.

Ironically, such problems may be inevitable. Rich people not only want to separate themselves from poorer people; they are also clearly attracted to other rich people. Expensive enclaves exist so they can hang out together. Exclusive golf clubs, ski clubs and sailing clubs serve this purpose. Not only do social clubs and fitness clubs have huge initiation fees (and other obstacles) to keep undesirables at bay, not only do they make rich people feel safely isolated, but they also make rich people (and perhaps some who can only just afford it) feel richer. And, of course, such places inevitably come with their own set of problems.

The Yellowstone Club, near Bozeman, Montana, is a case in point. Hacked out of the untouched wilderness, it bills itself as "the world's only private, members-only ski and golf community" and has an entire mountain to itself. Members included Bill Gates, Ben Affleck and Tom Brady. A who's who of the rich and famous built mansions there. And then it went bust after the 2008 financial crisis. A judge blamed the bank Credit Suisse for making sloppy and aggressive loans to various resorts, including the $375 million to Yellowstone and its developer, the lumber baron Tim Blixseth. An ugly legal battle ensued. Creditors accused Blixseth of spending most of the money not on the club, but to finance his own ridiculously lavish lifestyle, the usual toys and houses around the world. In 2012, a Montana bankruptcy judge ordered him to pay millions in restitution, but in 2014, Blixseth went to jail after telling an unconvinced judge he didn't have the money.

The dust has not yet settled. The bank denies any wrongdoing. Yellowstone creditors, who sought hundreds of millions from Blixseth, managed to get only $3 million. Blixseth himself sued Montana for forcing him into bankruptcy. And the members went back to enjoying a life of private luxury in the untamed wilds.

But they have not escaped all their challenges. In his book *Billionaire Wilderness*, psychologist Justin Farrell says the Yellowstone Club is a kind of hall of mirrors. The rich members are philanthropically inclined, ecologically minded and community driven, among other things, he writes. "Beneath the veneer, the reality of this institution and its use of nature and rural people involves raw economic interest, lasting environmental harm, and an intense culture of rural exclusion and militarized privacy."

Farrell spent five years in Teton County, Wyoming, what he calls the richest county in the richest country in the world, interviewing wealthy new residents and established country folk who help them make their vacation wilderness dreams come true. It all looks perfect, and for many newer residents it is just that. But issues remain. Rich people, Farrell concludes, often feel guilty and ungenuine, and they use philanthropy and environmental conservation to assuage their guilt while simultaneously and conveniently increasing their property values. They are attracted to these places, he writes, not just for the lifestyle, but also so they can feel more virtuous and authentic and use "nature and rural people as a vehicle for personal transformation."

Unfortunately for everyone, however, rural people in such places increasingly find it difficult to afford the cost of living amid the influx of all that money, much of it from hedge fund managers and dot-com billionaires. Even doctors and lawyers are increasingly priced out of vacation areas across the continent, not to mention big cities, tourist towns or scenic resort villages. The superrich, meanwhile, become insulated from (and less tolerant of) the more unpleasant realities of urban life—struggling businesses, empty storefronts, graffiti, litter and encampments.

Keeping Up Appearances

"Dishonesty, class loyalty and an absence of principle."
—George Monbiot, on what exclusive private schools breed

Reason No. 4 is that rich people struggle to stay rich.

Being rich, after all, is not cheap. Most people, when they get rich, start living the high life, travelling first class, eating well and buying a lot of stuff. And once you start spending, it's hard to stop. So there becomes the small matter of "maintaining a lifestyle." During her nasty and very public divorce from hedge fund billionaire Ken Griffin in 2015, Anne Dias Griffin outlined monthly expenses of $1 million. Nicole Young, the estranged wife of rapper Dr. Dre, told the court during her divorce case that she needed almost $2 million a month.

Whether they are throwing cash around like lottery winners or pinching pennies like Scrooge, sooner or later many rich people get poor. It's an inevitability for new money and old. It may take days, it may take generations, but it's coming as surely as a chuffing locomotive.

The banks are always circling, as any rich or poor person can confirm. And it's not just the banks. The journalist Robert Frank, in his alarming and fascinating book *The High-Beta Rich*, recounts —in cruelly hilarious detail—the exploits of repo men for the wealthy, and concludes: "There is an art to taking the prized possessions of the rich."

The desire for more—and better—is innate among our species. It's baked into our DNA. We want more money so we can buy more houses, clothes, cars. One never seems to be enough. Even ten, for some rich people, is just the beginning. It doesn't occur to us (until it's too late) that we're being greedy or overindulgent. More than a century ago, Thorstein Veblen, the legendary American economist and sociologist, coined the now-famous term to describe our addiction: conspicuous consumption.

Like squirrels before an approaching winter, we want this stuff because we fear, often with good reason, that it will someday run out. We can't really use it all, but it somehow gives us comfort, at least when we're buying it. We simply like being surrounded by possessions, whether they are useful or not. This may be why Taylor Swift owns eight homes, or why Floyd Mayweather at one time owned one hundred cars, or why Kylie Jenner has several hundred handbags in a room in her house dedicated to them.

Meanwhile, it is human nature to want to upgrade our surroundings, improve our conditions and innovate, which usually translates into more and better stuff. It's why moderately rich young people move from tiny starter homes into towering McMansions and finally into sprawling estates. Or suffer through expensive and trouble-prone kitchen and bathroom renovations while raising a family.

Unlike almost every other creature on the planet, humans appreciate art, whether it is a painting by Monet or a handbag by Balenciaga or a watch by Rolex. We see something in manufactured products and stuff that is more than the sum of its parts, and we want to be close to such items, to admire and fondle and, perhaps most importantly, display them for all to see. Apart from pack rats and a few birds, humans are the only creatures on Earth to worship stuff of no obvious use. Knick-knacks, conversation pieces, cushions. Even in useful items, we are always looking for something extra—colour, design, flair—to make our possessions stand out among the avalanche of stuff. It might be an iPhone or a Ferrari or a pair of Ferragamos. A faucet or a lampshade or a fridge. And each new design feature, every update, each new colour palette offered by retailers persuades us to unload the old item in white and replace it with one in silver or black.

As our tastes inevitably mature, our stuff gets better. For rich people, better is often bigger and more numerous and more expensive. YouTube is chockablock with rich people showing off their collections of outrageously expensive sneakers. Or handbags. Or watches. Mark Wahlberg may not have spent even $25 on his first watch, but according to the *Hollywood Reporter*, which calls him one of Hollywood's biggest watch collectors, he was spotted over the course of a single year in 2021 wearing eight different Rolexes and six by Patek Philippe, one of which, a twelve-complication Sky Moon Tourbillon, somehow retailed for more than half a million dollars. (But you probably couldn't find one for less than $1 million, if you could find one at all; see Reason No. 10). The fact that respectable news organizations such as the *Hollywood Reporter* (not to mention an entire genre of websites for collectors and the merely curious) are keeping track of such minutiae is one of the many peculiarities of our consumer society.

Humans are competitive, and envious. We compare ourselves with others (see Reason No. 5). We see what our friends, neighbours and colleagues have, we hear where they've been, and say to ourselves that we want that too. Humans want to belong, to be in the club, to regale people with stories of our exotic exploits. To do that, we need to maintain appearances, to keep up with the Kardashians and everyone else, whether we can afford it or not. And in the twenty-first century, as so many people seem to be getting forever richer, keeping up is getting more difficult. So when Wahlberg or a colleague or your friend shows off a million-dollar watch, or even a $10,000 watch, heaven forbid, the desire to have one like it is overwhelming, and the pressure on the bank accounts grows.

People spend money on more than just stuff; we spend it on services to make our lives easier and more enjoyable—and, more remarkable, to regale others with our exploits at cocktail parties and on social media. It goes without saying that anyone who buys a $10,000 watch (or even a $100 watch) is probably rich. But it's worth noting also that anyone who spends money on excessive services—transportation, accommodation or nutrition—is also by definition rich. The truly poor of this world simply do not have any help.

Most people who walk would love a bicycle. Most people who take the bus would love a lift in a car. Most people who take the subway are envious of those in limos, unless the limo is stuck in traffic. Most people who fly coach would love to sit in first class. Most people in first class secretly dream of travelling by private jet. And many people who can afford private jets hope one day to be floating weightless in a spaceship owned by Jeff Bezos or Elon Musk.

It never ends.

But these things are not cheap. Private planes require not only the millions to purchase them, but also expensive aviation fuel, pilots, maintenance staff, hangar fees and a flight attendant or two to serve drinks and snacks and open the doors and help store your bags and get you settled. And whatever the latest price tag is for experiencing weightlessness, it's a lot more than that of a private jet.

The sums rich people spend eating out makes the extravagant restaurant meals of three generations ago seem pedestrian by comparison. Steaks and wine and whisky keep getting allegedly better, and rich people simply have to sample it all, regardless of the price. Accommodation is the same. While average rich people are looking for hotel rooms at $200 a night, the stinking rich are in the Royal Suite at the Burj Al Arab in Dubai, which costs $28,000 a night. You can even spend $100,000 for a night in the Empathy Suite at the Palms in Las Vegas. When you are rich, it's easy to become poor, as many lottery winners and overnight sensations can attest.

As expensive as it is being rich, it can be even more expensive being famous. Celebrities not only need to stay rich, but they also need to stay famous if they are going to stay rich, so they need publicists and agents, expensive media campaigns and a lot of other helpers. And while rich people want private jets (who wouldn't?), famous people often say they *need* them to avoid annoying fans. They also need security systems and security huts at the end of their long driveways, and they need bodyguards to shoo away ordinary people. What to do?

Once again, rich people are well-advised to look for guidance from those who have been rich for generations. Old-monied folks know how expensive it is to be rich. They know being rich can be hard work (even if you don't have an actual job), and they have come up with schemes to mitigate the slow burn through savings, the endless leakage of cash for mundane but often expensive maintenance projects associated with aging estates and the attendant finery.

Old money also appreciates how glorious it is to be rich, and while they may not be able to relate to the misery of true poverty, they have come to understand, often through the experiences of friends, neighbours and ancestors, the humiliation of being poor after once being rich. Their friends shun them. Society ignores them. Poor people venture ever closer.

So what do rich people do to prevent this? They adopt certain strategies, which inevitably lead to problems.

First, rich people need to ensure their kids are also rich and will contribute, if at all possible, to the family fortune. They don't necessarily expect them to do any real work, of course, but more money is always helpful. They start by sending their kids to the right schools. The right schools are usually those that do not rely on the taxpayer to fund them, so they are expensive, but it's an investment. After all, such schools are full of other rich people's kids, and some of these classmates become friends for life, so kids who do not want to work much as adults can leverage these relationships when they become mediocre lawyers, investors or politicians (before they retire at thirty-five) and generate amounts of cash for which they would not otherwise qualify.

There is a long and storied history of the old-boy network in England, and other countries have been pretty good at copying it. But these networks create their own problems. To begin with, some of the most exclusive schools attract kids with money from far and wide, which means young people in attendance are separated from their parents for long periods. For some kids, this is ideal; for others, not so much. Some become unsupervised free spirits, others something darker; a few become victims of them.

Many rich people who went to boarding school have lived to regret it publicly. "Six horrible years" is how the infamous Huntington Hartford, once one of the world's richest men, described his experience as a boy at St. Paul's, an elite prep school in New Hampshire. An heir to the A&P supermarket chain, once one of the largest retail chains in the world, he later attended Harvard, but his expensive education appears to have been for naught. He managed to squander hundreds of millions of dollars during his now-infamous descent into debauchery and drug abuse.

Boris Johnson, the bumbling former British prime minister and London mayor, attended Eton, famously home for many years to royalty. "Like Boris Johnson, I was sent away," wrote George Monbiot, the British writer and environmental activist, in 2019. "These are institutions of fear, cruelty and trauma, and they create terrified bullies." Traits learned at such schools, wrote Monbiot, appear later in life: "Dishonesty, class loyalty and an absence of principle." Toronto's Upper Canada College produced some of the most famous members of the Canadian establishment. In *Old Boys: The Powerful Legacy of Upper Canada College,* journalist and author James FitzGerald hears from dozens of UCC grads, many of whom talk of the education and athletics, others about arrogance, elitism, wealth and physical and mental abuse. "You were at school with basically rich, white men," recalled John Schoeffel, who went there in the 1980s. "The greatest disservice the school did to me was not exposing me to the opinions and perspectives of women and other races." Avi Lewis attended in the 1970s: "I found that the people who came from the most wealth and power...were the most ruthless. Even at that young age, they carried with them the greatest sense of entitlement. They felt they deserved everything they got."

If you are the idle rich, and you want your children to follow in your footsteps, such traits are perhaps necessary. But getting into institutions of higher learning can be problematic. If your kids are smart, work hard, get good grades and behave themselves, accessing the right school is relatively easy. They simply apply like other rich kids. But it helps if your parents are really rich.

Jared Kushner, Donald Trump's son-in-law and former presidential whisperer who now runs a private equity firm mostly funded by the murderous Saudi Arabian crown prince Mohammed bin Salman, was accepted into Harvard University shortly after his father, now a convicted felon, had pledged $2.5 million to the place. The coincidence is one of many outlined in the book

The Price of Admission by Daniel Golden. Many rich students are not smart, do not work hard and do not behave themselves—that's a description that also befits many poor kids, of course, but rich kids, education or no, go on to be business and political leaders.

Rich people, Golden concludes, buy their way into elite colleges. That's what at least 750 families did between 2011 and 2018 in what has come to be known as the US College Admissions Scandal. As if university tuitions weren't already high enough, these families paid tens of thousands more to Rick Singer, who used some of the cash to inflate college entrance exam scores and bribe officials, including athletics staff and coaches. Maybe these parents simply wanted what was best for their kids. Maybe they wanted to give them a leg up. Maybe they were thinking about generational wealth. It was all for naught. A lot of rich people lost their money, including Mossimo Giannulli, a fashion designer, and his wife, Lori Loughlin, an actor famous for her roles on *Full House* and *When Calls the Heart*. Both were among those who also went to jail; their two daughters did not complete their studies at the University of Southern California.

The second thing the newly rich can do is emulate how old money marries. Arranged marriages may seem old-fashioned and callous, but they have their advantages, as many rich people can attest. Even poor people arrange marriages simply to survive poverty. Meanwhile, as any mother or father who is not too sentimental knows, you can fall in love with someone who's rich as easily as you can fall in love with someone who's poor (if falling in love even matters). Rich + rich generally equals richer. Poor + poor usually results in poor or poorer.

Moderately rich people often find marrying the right people advantageous. Somehow, many smart young rich people seem to know this. Perhaps they've been told by snotty (or stingy) parents, or perhaps they instinctively stay away or shun poor people. Let's face it: many rich people never even date people with different

backgrounds, let alone marry an outsider. It's only the true roman-
tics, rebels and free spirits who fall for some struggling artist,
musician or ne'er-do-well bartender, and if they do, rich parents
usually recognize it as a problem.

In 1916, F. Scott Fitzgerald wrote in his journal: "Poor boys
shouldn't think of marrying rich girls." That was after his relationship with Ginevra King, a society girlfriend he adored, ended, and
he put it in quotes, so many believe it came from her father. Mia
Farrow, as Daisy, would utter something similar to Robert Redford,
playing Jay Gatsby, in the 1974 movie based on Fitzgerald's book
The Great Gatsby. The basic principle doubtless guides many young
women and men today. "I've never actually dated outside my social
background, and I've thought about that, never," said Stephanie
Ercklentz, a twenty-something heiress interviewed in the 2003
documentary *Born Rich*. "It's really weird."

Ercklentz, who married a billionaire a few years later, never
required parental guidance on the matter; it apparently came naturally. Others, too, need no advice. Their own precarious wealth
sometimes makes a marriage of convenience a necessity. That's
how England found itself swimming in so-called Dollar Princesses
at the turn of the nineteenth century.

As the Gilded Age came to a close, British aristocrats were fabulously rich in terms of land holdings and estates, but they had
almost no spending cash. Their estates needed maintenance. They
needed to pay staff, and they couldn't be expected to work themselves
to make a living. These British aristocrats, who normally would
have turned up their noses at new money, looked to America for rich
brides, the daughters of newly wealthy manufacturers, railway
barons and miners who had struck it rich. The women, in turn,
were seeking status and lofty titles.

The fictional Lady Cora of television's *Downton Abbey* was
just such a person. So was Jennie Jerome, the mother of Winston

Churchill, in real life. In 1874, the Churchills were aghast at even the thought of a union with Jerome, the daughter of a rich American socialite, but her family paid a dowry equivalent to several millions today, so they decided to grin and bear it. Railroad heiress Consuelo Vanderbilt married the Duke of Marlborough. Lord Curzon agreed to marry dry-goods heiress Mary Leiter. And who could know at the time that Frances Ellen Work, who married James Boothby Burke Roche, would be the great-grandmother of the Princess of Wales— otherwise known as Lady Diana? Class barriers, so rigid for so many years, were easily overcome by economic reality.

Cinderella stories do sometimes happen in real life. Rich royals do occasionally rescue poor commoners from poverty, but even two hundred years after Jane Austen created the memorable Mr. Darcy in her 1813 novel *Pride and Prejudice,* marrying up—or down —remains a challenge for the rich as much as for the poor. Humans have always been afraid of "the other," and if you are rich, "the other" is often poor people, or even those who are simply not as rich as you.

Early on in civilization, and probably before, humans every-where developed, consciously or unconsciously, a class system— dividing society between the haves and the have-nots—to separate themselves from poor people, or simply to bolster their own egos. Rich people kept poor people at a distance, unless they needed help, in which case they kept them close indeed (see Reason No. 2). They invented clubs where they decided who could join (rich men) and who could not (everyone else). They built grand estates far from prying eyes, travelled by private rail cars or personal jets.

So the civilized world long ago was separated into four groups: those with social and economic status (old money); those with social status but deteriorating economic fortunes (tired money); those with economic status only (new money); and those with neither (poor people). For millennia, those with both money and social status have been struggling to keep it while everyone else has been clamouring for a better position for themselves and their children.

It's why, for most of the twentieth century, ambitious poor couples across North America, where there was never supposed to be a class system, aspired to move out of ever-changing urban working-class neighbourhoods to more homogeneous and predictable suburbias, where racism, unwritten rules and a lack of public transit kept poorer people and recent immigrants away.

Suburbia wasn't for the superrich, of course, but it was the place where you could convince yourself that you were sort of rich, where everyone had similar middle-class incomes, or pretended they did. They dressed the same, talked the same, and went to the same parties and sporting events. They aspired to the same things. Their kids got to go to schools with other increasingly rich people, and thus make their way up the economic and social ladder, which, in many of the richer cities by the end of the century, meant moving back downtown, where the public transit and restaurants were better.

But while old-monied rich people have their vices, and their endless problems, many no longer feel obliged to keep up with the neighbours, perhaps due to privations and problems resulting from such indulgences in the past. Or perhaps because they've been at it so long that the novelty has worn off. They are content to drive modest vehicles. Their homes are grand but not constantly renovated. They're not overly fussed about peeling paint, as long as it's kept to a minimum. It's true, some take up expensive hobbies like sailing or car racing, but many are content to garden or paint. Old-monied rich people may buy expensive liquor and wine, perhaps, but they don't swill it ostentatiously. They don't ring up huge dinner bills at the latest trendy restaurant, and they never, ever pick up the tab in a flourish of generosity. They may attend cocktail soirees to have fun or keep up appearances, but many of them know better than to blow their fortunes on late-night indulgences and mindless partying.

At some point, most rich people come to the realization that spending extravagantly loses its lustre after a prolonged period. Stuff piles up, and exotic travel arrangements seem more trouble than staying home, where you can get a good night's sleep in your own bed and a piece of toast and a cup of tea in the morning. They learn at some point that the grass is not necessarily greener elsewhere, and that FOMO (fear of missing out) is not a sustainable philosophy.

Never Enough

Reason No. 5 is that rich people generally want to be richer.

This—believe it or not—is different from Reason No. 4. The point is not what the money can buy, but simply the thrill of numbers and the growing pot. Like the gambler who can never win enough. Or Ebenezer Scrooge, the famous miser in Charles Dickens's A Christmas Carol, who spent his days counting money and complaining about people having fun until he realized there was more to life than tallying up shillings. Many observers believe Dickens's character was inspired by the British property developer and politician John Elwes, known as "Elwes the Miser." A rich man who died a multimillionaire by today's standards, he captured the imagination of Dickens and attracted the wrath of his compatriots, but he wasn't alone, even then.

Thomas Cooke, who lived in the same era, was so famously cheap that a book was published about him in 1814, three years after his death, entitled The Life of Mr. Thomas Cooke, Late of Pentonville (A Miser), by William Chamberlaine. Born into poverty, Cooke married a wealthy widow, acquired all her money, set out in various businesses, acted cruelly and died obscenely rich in old age. According to Chamberlaine: "His avarice increased with his income."

Fictional money hoarders have been a regular part of writers' imaginations for centuries, from Shakespeare's Shylock to George Eliot's Silas Marner. Ben Jonson, Molière, Alexander Pope and Robert Louis Stevenson all produced them.

When I was a boy, one of my favourite comic-book characters was Scrooge McDuck, created in 1947 for the Walt Disney Company. The fabulously rich Scottish uncle of the iconic Donald Duck, he was conceived merely as a one-time interloper, but became so popular he got his own comic-book series and still lives today in print and animated films. I remember vividly his nephews, Huey, Dewey and Louie, frolicking in their uncle's vault amid mounds of cash, diving into rolling hills of dollar bills, swimming through it like kids in the ball pit at a McDonald's play area. It looked glorious. McDuck lived for money. He was fabulously rich, and frugal, and he had all the cash anyone could ever need, yet he still wanted more. Indeed, his raison d'être was to go on adventures and find more money.

To me, it all seemed perfectly logical. In junior school, I had envied all those kids with huge bags of marbles or stacks of baseball cards. I could never manage to accumulate more than a few dog-eared duds myself, and I really had no idea why I wanted more. After all, what good were they? But I knew this: my schoolmates seemed to respect those few who had lots. I did not give any thought at the time to the inconvenience they presented, the space they took up in a knapsack, or the weight of it all on those long walks down a dirt road to school. Indeed, other than status, they brought nothing but problems.

And so, when my parents helped me open a bank account early in life, it seemed the next logical step. I would add my allowance to it, if there was anything left after Popsicles and penny candy.

Later, I would take my meagre earnings from a paper route, make the long walk to the local bank, and place the profits in the account. I had a little blue balance book in which the bank teller wrote, just like Scrooge, my net worth. This book was somehow important to me. I kept it close, reviewed it regularly. It was all, of course, part of my parents' plan—to instill in me some responsibility for my own finances and to introduce me, perhaps, to the value of saving and the concept of interest, which the bank was adding to my account, then as now, in mere pennies. I may even have dreamed that one day, perhaps, I would have mountains of money like McDuck.

I was likely not alone, but today, most of us are trained not to save but to spend. Our bank balances are important, sure, but it's the credit card statements that hang over us like dark clouds, the mortgage payments that loom, the interest rates we pay that make headlines. Even for most rich people, life is a constant struggle to balance revenue and expenses.

A growing segment of rich people do not have this concern but have taken it up anyway. Their bank balances are still important to them, tens or hundreds of millions of dollars later. Like many rich people, they are motivated by both greed and envy: they want something more. They don't want what money can buy; they want the money itself. They want more of it to count, to contemplate, to grow, to worship. They do not want to be rich to spend the money, enjoy a life of leisure or glamour, own expensive things, donate to charities, change the world or even help friends and family; they simply want to be richer. They don't have time for all the trappings of wealth, as they spend all their time at work. The money is no longer the object; it is the perceived power that comes with it that they seek. They define themselves by their money, and eventually by the size of their fortune.

Two of the richest men in history, the famous robber barons J. Pierpont Morgan and John D. Rockefeller, are remembered both as misers and as philanthropists—and they loved money for its own sake. Rockefeller, the famous founder of Standard Oil, once confided in a neighbour in Cleveland: "Do you know the only thing that gives me pleasure? It's to see my dividends coming in." Morgan, a contemporary who revolutionized banking in America and indeed the world, was equally obsessed with cash for cash's sake. "Money to him," wrote a biographer, J.R. MacGregor, "was like a natural resource that could be harnessed and utilized" to make more money.

Jeffrey Winters, a political science professor at Northwestern University and the author of *Oligarchy*, describes oligarchs as people who "use money to make money" and are obsessed with what he calls "wealth defence." "Every billionaire I've spoken to, and I've spoken to quite a number of them, is extremely excited by each additional increment of money they make."

In pursuit of such gratuitous and boundless wealth, many oligarchs have succumbed to workaholism. Not for them the idle, aristocratic life of a nineteenth-century Englishman. Antonio García Martínez, author of *Chaos Monkeys: Obscene Fortune and Random Failure in Silicon Valley*, says that "they simply can't stop doing it. They derive transcendent meaning from capitalism. Without their money, what else would they have?"

Roy Thomson, the Canadian newspaper magnate and the 1st Baron Thomson of Fleet, once explained, "I buy newspapers to make money, to buy more newspapers to make more money." Thomson was once asked for the secret to his success: "No leisure, no pleasure, just work."

Thomson's grandson may feel differently. A business executive who has helped grow the family company exponentially since the days of his grandfather, David Thomson rarely speaks to the media, but is said to have, well, wider interests than just work and money. "When you try to live a more balanced life, traditional businessmen think that you are not a true man," Thomson told James

FitzGerald in *Old Boys: The Powerful Legacy of Upper Canada College*. "But who is not the real man? You are telling me? You have not taken a weekend with your wife, you have no spare time that you use constructively, you do not have any hobbies. You do not know how to spell Mozart and here you are telling me that I am weak?"

Indeed, for every two rich people who worship money, there may be another one who finds that a problem. The early American industrialist Andrew Carnegie was particularly anxious about the issue. "The amassing of wealth is one of the worse species of idolatry," he wrote. "No idol more debasing than the worship of money."

The problem is that when you fall prey to that idolatry, no amount of money is ever going to be enough. The former president of the United States Donald Trump is such a person. Yes, he obviously likes to show off his stuff, but showing off the money itself is far more important. Fond of telling people "I'm really rich," in 2009 he sued Timothy O'Brien, author of the 2005 book *TrumpNation: The Art of Being the Donald*, which states that Trump, well-known even then for embellishment if not the outright lies that would later make him infamous worldwide, had a fortune of $150 million to $250 million. Trump was incensed by the alleged underestimate: "It's indisputable," he said, insisting his net worth is in the billions, not merely hundreds of millions. Most observers just rolled their eyes. The judge threw the case out.

Let's say Trump has $250 million, or even $2.5 billion, an estimate made by *Forbes* in 2023. It's an awful lot of money, but it's still not enough for Trump, who has insisted in the past his net worth is $10 billion or more. Some say his long-running battle with the government (and the media) to keep his tax records secret was not because of alleged tax avoidance, but simply because the records would reveal he wasn't as rich as he has so often boasted.

Most observers are flummoxed by Trump's need to inflate almost everything he has and does, but rich people who care about money for money's sake, who crave the attention it generates and the respect it engenders, may understand. Money is power, and more money means more power. That's why Trump, like so many other rich people, doesn't like paying taxes, or even many of his bills (see Reason No. 7), let alone giving to needy charities—it lowers his net worth, and therefore his power.

In fact, Trump used his charitable foundation for business and political purposes instead of just philanthropy. At a charity auction, he spent $20,000 of the foundation's money, most of it donated by other people, to buy a six-foot portrait of himself, and another $12,000 for an autographed football helmet, among other things. In 2018, he agreed to shut the foundation down and pay more than $2 million in court-ordered damages. The New York attorney general alleged the foundation had engaged in "persistently illegal conduct."

Perhaps this kind of behaviour is key to Trump's success with so many at the extremes of the Republican Party. He is acting like a poor person but posing as a rich person. He doesn't have any qualms about penny-pinching any more than he worries about lying or cheating. Unlike some rich people, who try (often unsuccessfully) to be discreet about their wealth, he flaunts his like nobody else. Luxury, extravagance, opulence, grandeur and excess are his trademarks, and while many people are appalled, an equal number, apparently, are suitably impressed.

On the other end of the (admittedly narrow) spectrum sits Warren Buffett, the so-called Oracle of Omaha, who has made $100 billion, give or take several billion, through value investing. He lives a relatively modest life for someone so rich. Not one inclined to acquire Trump's gilded trophies and status symbols, he inhabits the same house he bought in Omaha in 1958 for $31,500. He still drives to work every day (in his Cadillac, which he replaces every six or seven years). He laments the fact that he doesn't pay *enough* taxes. He has often said people should "leave the children enough so that they can do anything, but not enough that they can do nothing."

Still, watching money grow is what thrills him the most. Not the power or prestige that Trump seeks, but simply the art of it all. For Buffett, compound interest at work is performance art, a thing to behold. He cares about the bottom line, obviously, but is fascinated by the process and the power of interest paid on savings. That doesn't mean the mountains of cash he controls are any less obscene, nor does it condone or condemn his obsession with money in a world with so many challenges, but it seems more interesting, and Buffett has more admirers than most billionaires (see Reason No. 8).

A quarter of a century ago, I attended the annual meeting of Buffett's holding company, Berkshire Hathaway. Back then, it was attended by a mere eleven thousand people. Now known far and wide as "Woodstock for Capitalists," this orgiastic celebration of profit and free enterprise now attracts more than forty thousand people, many of them shareholders, to Omaha each year.

Once there, they shop gleefully for products produced by Berkshire Hathaway companies, they talk about the price of the stock, and finally, they sit in rapt attention as Buffett and his partner, Charlie Munger, now ninety-nine years old, sit on a stage *for more than six hours*, answering questions from shareholders, drinking Cherry Coke and eating See's chocolates, among other products in which the vaunted company has an interest. Most of those in attendance simply want to hear the great money wizards wax financial. Some are trying to learn more about value investing. And some just want to make more money. "They'll go down in history," said Gavin Cretsinger at the 2022 meeting. "To see them in the flesh, that's pretty incredible."

Both Munger and Buffett have often counselled against what motivates many rich people. "The world is not driven by greed,"

Munger has often said, "it's driven by envy." Greed is defined as a strong desire for more—more wealth, possessions, power—than a person needs. Envy is the feeling of wanting something that somebody else has. Somewhere between them swirls the vortex in which people often find themselves lost, unable to pull away.

From the fictional character Gordon Gekko in the movie *Wall Street*, to every snake-oil salesman from Charles Ponzi to Bernie Madoff, it is human nature to want more, whether we need it or not. "You see a little of that in the athletic field and the entertainment field and perhaps even on Wall Street," laments Buffett. "Making a million dollars a year looks great until this guy that sits next to you that can't possibly be as smart as you is making a million too, and then the whole world turns into a very unfair place."

This is not unique to millionaires. Moderately rich people and poor people compare themselves with friends, neighbours and colleagues. We feel we should have what others have (or slightly more) and we judge our success not against most of the world but within the confines of our small social and professional circles. This problem is particularly serious for the superrich, and perhaps because the figures are often so impressive and the people involved so famous, if only for being rich, it often becomes a matter of public record.

That's why we hear so much about what actors or athletes are paid, and how much others demand, or tawdry stories about the size of trailers on location for Hollywood movies. So despite all the lessons from religious leaders, Victorian novelists and aging billionaires, the supply of hoarders and misers and McDucks, already apparently inexhaustible, is unlikely to dry up any time soon.

While many rich people have guilt about their great good luck, others have had quite enough of the whole "let's hammer the rich" movement. "One thing I'm not is humble anymore, I'm sick of being humble," announced Catherine Zeta-Jones, the movie star married to movie star Michael Douglas, in 2018. "So sorry

I'm rich, so sorry I'm married to a movie star, so sorry I'm not bad looking. No sorrys. Enough."

Simone Grace Seol is among those who says hallelujah to that. The South Korea–based author and business mentor, who hosts the podcast *Joyful Marketing*, says it's time for the world to lighten up. "The idea of just making money for the sake of money is legitimate and honourable and should be deshamed."

Shame does not appear to be a problem for modern rappers such as NBA YoungBoy, DaBaby, Trippie Redd, Jon Geezy and Parlae, who apparently set stacks of cash on fire because...well, it's not exactly clear. Neither is it evident whether the cash was fake, but making a show of it, wasteful or not, tends to raise one's status, if only in one's own eyes. Money to burn is not just an expression but an aspiration. Uncontrolled spending is always a good show, but there is nothing more evocative or demonstrative than having so much you can afford to watch it go up in flames.

For less brazen rich people, one way to deal with large, abstract sums of money—and to show off how much is at their disposal—is to give it away.

Appalled by his own obscene fortune at a young age, Andrew Carnegie promised to resign at age thirty-five to commit himself to philanthropy. "To continue much longer overwhelmed by business cares and with most of my thoughts wholly upon the way to make money in the shortest time, must degrade me beyond hope of permanent recovery," he wrote. Before that, though, he spent many years as a brutal boss who exploited his workers, and perhaps predictably didn't carry through with his philanthropic plans until his mid-forties, a decade overdue by his own reckoning. But when he did, he went at it with a vengeance. When Carnegie died more than three decades later, he had given away the bulk of his $400 million fortune, the equivalent of $5 billion today, funding the establishment of almost three thousand libraries worldwide, among other things.

In 2010, Warren Buffett and his billionaire buddy Bill Gates created the Giving Pledge, "a promise by the world's wealthiest individuals and families to dedicate the majority of their wealth to charitable causes," which today has been signed by more than two hundred people, mostly billionaires, across the globe, including Elon Musk, Larry Ellison, Mark Zuckerberg and Priscilla Chan. At ninety-two, Buffett has given away about $50 billion.

But giving away their riches, even if they want to, is a problem for some billionaires. In 2017, Jeff Bezos famously asked followers on Twitter for suggestions on how to donate cash, apparently prompted by questions from the *New York Times* about his philanthropic plans. Bezos has often said he was never motivated by money, but makes tons of it nonetheless, and now he may feel obliged by public opinion to disperse some of it. Although Bezos has now given away more than $2 billion, according to *Forbes*, he is still not even approaching the traditional definition of tithing.

A concept that predated Jesus Christ and has guided the devout of various religions for millennia, tithing literally means "one-tenth," and that portion—of land, food, money, whatever—is what many religious institutions have expected followers to donate. Philanthropy, from the ancient Greek meaning "love of humanity," may have been a human trait since we were hunter-gatherers. But carrying through with it is complicated, apparently, in a modern world with so much money and so much need.

"It's not easy," Bezos told CNN in an interview with his partner, Lauren Sánchez, in 2022. "Building Amazon was not easy. It took a lot of hard work, a bunch of very smart teammates, hard-working teammates, and I'm finding—and I think Lauren is finding the same thing—that charity, philanthropy, is very similar."

Interestingly, Bezos's ex-wife, billionaire novelist MacKenzie Scott, is having no such trouble. By contrast, she is setting a philanthropic pace unmatched in modern times, perhaps in history. Unlike her ex, she has signed the Giving Pledge, and, according to *Forbes*, she has given away almost $15 billion since 2020, and has turned the business of philanthropy on its head. She gave a $55-million estate in Beverly Hills to the California Community Foundation. Habitat for Humanity received almost half a billion dollars. She gave $2.7 billion to organizations that fight against wealth inequality. And it looks as if she's just started. "My approach to philanthropy will continue to be thoughtful," Scott wrote in her letter to the Giving Pledge. "It will take time and effort and care. But I won't wait. And I will keep at it until the safe is empty."

And Laurene Powell Jobs, the widow of Apple's founder, Steve Jobs, was involved in philanthropy before she met her husband, and before she became one of the richest women in the world after his death in 2011. Her late husband, she says, "didn't care about the accumulation of wealth," which is probably correct. He cared about Apple, about design and aesthetics, about changing the world, but he didn't seem to care personally about the stuff money could buy or the power (beyond Apple) that it could bestow. Powell Jobs hasn't signed the Giving Pledge but has committed nonetheless to giving away her vast fortune as soon as she can. "It's not right for individuals to accumulate a massive amount of wealth that's equivalent to millions and millions of other people combined," she said. "There's nothing fair about that."

Obviously, there are more rich women today, and they have more money, but the growing trend of high-profile women philanthropists may also be illuminated by studies finding that girls are likely to be more prosocial than boys—or more likely to go out of their way to help others, including strangers. *Forbes* estimates men give away only about half as much of their wealth as women. A study by the Women's Philanthropy Institute at the School of Philanthropy at Indiana University found more women than men in every income bracket give to charity. "Women overall are more likely to give, and give more, than men," the researchers concluded. What role did Melinda French Gates play in her husband's shift from mere billionaire entrepreneur to a philanthropic tour de force? He arrived on the list of the ten richest people in the world in 1991, reached the top of it in 1995, and held that spot well into the new century. The Bill & Melinda Gates Foundation, one of the biggest charities in the world, was launched in 2000. Was it simply all that money piling up that made Gates more philanthropic? Or did French Gates play more than just a key role in the partnership?

Whatever the reason, he is all-in today. As a founder of the Giving Pledge, he often reminds other billionaires of their duty to give, and give big. In 2022, Gates announced the foundation would step up spending from $6 billion a year to $9 billion a year to fight disease and poverty around the world, among other things. "As I look to the future," Gates said, "I plan to give virtually all of my wealth to the foundation. I will move down and eventually off the list of the world's richest people."

Some observers wonder if that is enough. Yvon Chouinard, the founder and majority owner of Patagonia, the hugely successful clothing company, has already outdone them all. In 2022, he gave the company, valued at about $3 billion, to an environmental non-profit and placed its voting stock in a trust. About $100 million in profits annually will now be used to combat climate change and protect undeveloped land across the planet. "Hopefully this will influence a new form of capitalism that doesn't end up with a few rich people and a bunch of poor people," said Chouinard when the donation made headlines. A rock climber and outdoors enthusiast who eschews most of the traditional trappings of wealth, he was inspired to give everything away when a 2017 article in *Forbes* labelled him a billionaire and "it really pissed me off. I don't have a billion dollars in the bank. I don't drive Lexuses." In his note to employees announcing the gift, he said, "Earth is now our only shareholder."

Chouinard's decision has attracted a lot of attention—and represents an extreme philanthropy that remains rare. "Even those who have signed the Giving Pledge," says David Callahan, founder of Inside Philanthropy, a website that follows philanthropic trends, "don't give away that much, and tend to get richer every year."

Grifters, Bill Collectors and Relatives

"*I was much happier when I was broke.*"
—William "Bud" Post, who won $16 million in a lottery

Reason No. 6 is that everyone wants some of rich people's money.

Most people worry about making money; rich people worry about keeping it. Poor people panic about having enough to eat. Moderately rich people fret about a hike in the mortgage rate.

But the truly rich have bigger money issues, at least as far as they are concerned. They may be mildly upset about the about ups and downs in the stock market, buying a yacht that's too small or bidding foolishly on some worthless art, but what really concerns them are fees and filchers. They've got a lot to lose.

This is less of a concern for poor people. I once volunteered for a few years in a soup kitchen at a local church: making dinner, serving food, chatting with guests. Many visitors were of limited means with few possessions. Some didn't have enough winter clothes, and in the coldest months, I'd often hand out mittens, hats and coats that had been donated to those facing a frigid walk home or a night on the streets. Many would return a week later without the stuff we gave them a week earlier, and I soon realized that when food and shelter are scarce, possessions can be more ephemeral.

Rich people don't have to worry about their basic needs. But they do worry about their stuff and who might take it from them. That's why they install expensive alarm systems, video equipment, uncrackable safes or security huts. That's why they fret more than most about looters and thieves. And why not? Rich people are exactly those targeted by such criminals, sometimes for philosophical reasons, but mostly because the pickings are so good.

One famous cat burglar is Blane David Nordahl, a career criminal who cut a swath across the American Northeast for four decades, from 1983 to 2013. When he was arrested in 1996 (ironically travelling with two cats—and a directory of the rich and famous), prosecutors said his specialty was stolen silver. It was alleged he had taken 120 pairs of silver salt-and-pepper shakers from the Greenwich home of Ivana Trump.

Coincidentally, Ivana Trump was mentioned in the earlier memoir of another famous cat burglar, Peter Scott, a British man who billed himself as a modern-day Robin Hood. Scott stole from Elizabeth Taylor, Sophia Loren and Lauren Bacall, among others, and authorities estimated he took material worth more than £30 million between the 1950s and 1980s. "The people I burgled got rich through greed and skullduggery," he would write in *Gentleman Thief* in 1995. "They indulged in the mechanics of ostentation— they deserved me and I deserved them. If I rob Ivana Trump, it is just a meeting of two different types of degeneracy on a dark rooftop."

It's not just pickpockets, muggers and burglars, but pretty much everyone, including other rich people, that worry rich people. Successful entrepreneurs, tech billionaires and fortunate heirs must always be on the lookout for litigious colleagues, greedy assistants (see Reason No. 2), needy acquaintances, crafty interlopers and alleged friends. And it's no wonder, given their various misfortunes and misadventures, and the endless demands placed on them by lesser folk. Many of these relationships, familial or financial, inevitably disintegrate into bitter feuds because, well, there's apparently never enough money to go around, no matter how much you have.

Actor and entrepreneur Gwyneth Paltrow experienced this kind of misery following a skiing collision between her and a rich stranger, Terry Sanderson, on the slopes of the luxurious Deer Valley Resort in Utah in 2016. Sanderson, a retired optometrist, sued Paltrow, Paltrow countersued, and the case came to court in 2023, an often cringe-worthy televised event that became a brief but very public spectacle before a jury found Sanderson "100 per cent" at fault. Paltrow was awarded $1 and reimbursed for the legal fees in her countersuit, and Sanderson regretted the entire episode: "I'm gonna be on the internet forever."

No celebrity, if they are perceived to have any money at all, is safe from litigious strangers. Media star Oprah Winfrey fended off a lawsuit by Texas cattlemen after she swore off hamburgers; singer and actor Jennifer Lopez was sued by a flight attendant who said Lopez's guard dog attacked her; and Miley Cyrus was sued by a Los Angeles woman who said what Cyrus described as making a "goofy face" in a photograph violated the rights of Asian Pacific Islanders. She said Cyrus owed some one million people $4,000 each. Cyrus apologized; the case was dismissed.

Lottery winners, too, learn quickly that all that money comes with problems—often from other people who want some of it. At first, it's thrilling. The stuff they can buy, the places they can go, the parties they can host. Unfortunately, studies show lottery winners are not necessarily any happier than losers, and they derive less joy from things like hanging out with friends or simply watching TV. Jay Sommers, who won $5 million in the Michigan state lottery in 1988, was an early student in this respect. Years later, he would ironically sum up the big win as the experience that "ruined" his life: "Everybody expected money from me," he told the *New York Post*.

"I had uncles expecting and friends (wanting money) that I don't even speak to anymore."

Those who hit the jackpot are so predictably deluged by requests for money that experts recommend the first thing they do after depositing the cheque is skip the country for six months. Despite that advice—and dozens of sob stories from previous lottery winners—Jack Whittaker chose another route. A West Virginia business owner who won more than $100 million in 2002, he revelled in the celebrity of his newfound wealth. He made himself available to the media, appeared on television frequently, and announced to the world he planned to give away much of the money. Indeed, he would shower family members with treasure, give money to the clerk who sold him the winning ticket, buy a house for the waitress at his favourite diner, build a new local church and assist needy strangers who asked for help: "I want to promote goodwill and help people."

It didn't go as planned. Everyone had an idea of how Whittaker should spend the staggering sum. Poor people stalked him. A few threatened his family. He had to hire deputies from the local sheriff's office for security. He employed a team to open letters begging for cash. And he needed a private investigator to separate the paupers from the grifters. By 2003, his foundation, inundated by requests, had to suspend operations. His marriage fell apart. He spoiled his teenage granddaughter Brandi, but she slipped into a life of debauchery and drug abuse. Two years after he bought the winning ticket, she was dead under mysterious circumstances. "She was my world," a devastated Whittaker told a reporter.

And Whittaker himself? The God-fearing local hero became a changed man, lording his millions over poor locals, flashing wads of cash indiscriminately, drinking to excess, acting belligerently, alienating friends and sexually harassing female bartenders and patrons at local drinking establishments. Misty Dawn Arnold, who worked at the local strip joint that Whittaker began frequenting, told the *Washington Post* in 2018 that nothing good came of the windfall. "It was like the money was eating away at whatever was good in him."

He had a habit of carrying vast quantities of cash, and thieves once removed more than half a million dollars he had inexplicably kept in his Lincoln when it was parked outside a strip club. He was sued by (among others) Caesars Atlantic City for bouncing $1.5 million worth of cheques (see Reason No. 7). He was charged with drunk driving. And, of course, he tired of the media attention (see Reason No. 1): "I tell everybody my personal life is my own business."

Whittaker's story is not unique. There are more tales of winning woes than hopeful gamblers care to admit. William "Bud" Post was awarded more than $16 million in a 1988 Pennsylvania lottery, a windfall that was particularly timely for the poverty-stricken drifter who had served time in jail for writing bad cheques. He bought two homes, several cars, a truck, two motorcycles, a sailboat and an airplane, though he did not possess a pilot's licence. He gave money to his siblings, two brothers and a sister. But it all went so wrong so fast. Within a year, he was estranged from his siblings and was ordered to stay away from his sixth wife after he shot at her car with a rifle. His brother, meanwhile, tried to hire a contract killer to murder them both.

And Post himself was sent to jail for assault. Ironically, the newly minted millionaire somehow faced cash-flow problems, as well as the predictable array of house-maintenance problems, legal problems, health problems, relationship problems and more. Eight years later, he wanted nothing to do with any of it: "Once I'm no longer a lottery winner, people will leave me alone. That's all I want. Just peace of mind." On the matter of money, he said this: "I was much happier when I was broke."

None of that, however, can compare to the tragic story of Jeffrey Dampier. A security guard in Chicago, he won $20 million in the

Illinois Lottery in 1996. He quit his job, moved to Tampa, opened a small business, and settled down to a comfortable life, sharing his wealth with his new wife and her family. But it would soon end badly. He had an affair with his wife's sister, Victoria Jackson, who then kidnapped him with her boyfriend, tied him up in the back of a van and shot him dead. After she had been convicted of murder by a jury, Jackson turned to her mother and made an unlikely assumption: "Jeffrey forgives me."

It was a tragic and unusual end for a lottery winner, but kidnapping remains a constant concern for rich people. Harrowing tales from the not-so-distant past still haunt us all. The aviation hero Charles Lindbergh is remembered for many things, good and bad, but perhaps most for the devasting death of his two-year-old son at the hands of kidnappers in 1932.

In 1963, Frank Sinatra Jr., son of the famous crooner, was returned after kidnappers were paid $240,000. Decades later, in 1998, following an article in the *Los Angeles Times*, one of the kidnappers, by then having served his time and re-emerged a millionaire realtor, was offered $1.5 million to recount the story for a film. Frank Jr. filed a lawsuit to stop it. He won the case—finally—based on a law preventing criminals from profiting from their crimes.

The avaricious industrialist J. Paul Getty—once so paranoid about being taken advantage of that he installed a payphone for guests in his sprawling mansion—famously refused to pay a $17-million ransom when his grandson was taken in Rome in 1973 because he worried it would encourage more kidnappings of family members. After he finally agreed to finance some of it, a ransom of $3 million was paid, his grandson was returned, minus one ear, and the young man promptly descended into alcohol and drug abuse.

In 1971, kidnappers ransomed frugal billionaire Theo Albrecht for about $2 million. When the kidnappers were arrested but only half the money recovered, Albrecht, the owner of the huge discount supermarket chain Aldi, tried, without success, to claim the loss as a business expense. Always media shy, Albrecht, once famously described by *Forbes* as "more reclusive than a Yeti," disappeared behind the walls of his fortress-like home, avoiding photographers and the media until he died in 2010. His heirs have been fighting over the fortune ever since. "The conflict, which has been through many chapters," wrote David Dawkins of *Forbes* in 2020, "pits the cost-conscious elders who built Aldi against the younger generation who inherited the wealth."

In 1983, Freddy Heineken, head of the famous Dutch brewery, was ransomed for 35 million Dutch guilders. After that, he hired more bodyguards, used an armoured car for commuting and buttressed security at his house. Speaking to a biographer, he sounded a note familiar to many rich and famous people: "The nice thing about being rich is that you can fly to the Caribbean whenever you want... but I can't even go to an Amsterdam cinema."

Heineken's was one of the largest known ransom payments in history until 1996, when Victor Li Tzar-kuoi, the teenage son of Hong Kong billionaire Li Ka-shing, was ransomed for HK $1 billion. (The kidnapper later called Li for advice on how to invest the money.)

In 2005, police foiled a kidnapping plot aimed at the sixteen-month-old son of funnyman David Letterman at his sprawling ranch in Montana. Such incidents cannot be easy on victims and their families, and they are a painful reminder to rich people that they can never quite let down their guard. Statistics, while unreliable, show kidnapping remains a threat worldwide. Travel advisories warn regularly about such places as South Africa, Mexico, Venezuela, Colombia, the Philippines, Brazil, Lebanon, Pakistan and Turkey. No wonder so many companies offer kidnapping and ransom insurance ("K&R" for short). For insurance companies, it's another way to legitimately extract money from rich people who might otherwise have it illegitimately extracted from them, a pay-me-now or pay-them-later proposition.

Relatives are a joy for most of us, but a problem for many, whether they're getting themselves kidnapped, besmirching the family name or just making trouble at Thanksgiving dinner. There's often some sibling or cousin who needs more cash, and a few who simply *want* more. But for rich people, there are family members who *demand* more, and won't take no for an answer—and often an equal number of rich people unwilling to bend to even the most reasonable requests. These are ex-spouses and children, too, and rich people often seem to have a lot of both.

The list of rich people who refuse to appropriately support spouses and children is alarmingly long. For most of history, they simply ejected inconvenient kinfolk from the household, and abandoned them to a life of poverty, homelessness and misery. On occasion, particularly troublesome wives were beheaded by their powerful husbands.

The situation has improved, obviously, but many modern deadbeat dads go to great lengths to minimize their obligations. The late Jack Kent Cooke, a stingy Canadian-American billionaire who in the 1990s owned Manhattan's Chrysler Building and the football team now known as the Washington Commanders, among various other expensive toys, fathered a child at seventy-four but refused to admit it. A nasty court battle ensued between Cooke and his thirty-three-year-old Ex-Wife No. 3, whom Cooke's lawyers took to verbally attacking. One termed her "an odalisque—that's better than a trollop" and alleged the child support was in fact "disguised alimony."

Eventually, Cooke was forced to concede paternity and paid $2,420 a month in child support, a figure that was doubled in 1995, neither of which put even a noticeable dent in his obscene fortune. Such payments, said the judge at the time, were determined by the parent's income, not net worth. For her part, his ex had this to say:

"I just hope what her father has done to her is not going to affect her later in life. I will never say anything bad about Jack to her. I will say 'Your father was very sick and is to be pitied more than anything.'"

John Paul Getty Jr., jet-setting heroin addict and son of the infamous oil baron and miser, initially refused to pay medical expenses for his son John Paul Getty III, who had been famously kidnapped (and lost an ear) years earlier, suffered trauma as a result, and overdosed on alcohol and drugs, causing paralysis and partial blindness. Getty Jr. was raking in more than $20 million a year from the family trust, but his ex-wife had to sue him for $25,000 a month to pay for her son's medical expenses. The judge was appalled.

In 1978, Steve Jobs, the maniacally fastidious founder of Apple Inc., fathered a child he denied was his until the district attorney of San Mateo County, California, forced DNA tests that proved otherwise. At the time, his daughter, Lisa Brennan-Jobs, was supported by welfare payments and income her mother received from waitressing and cleaning houses. In 1980, just days before Apple went public and Jobs learned he was worth more than $200 million, his lawyers pushed for a deal, and Jobs agreed to child-support payments of $500 a month.

In her acclaimed 2018 memoir, Brennan-Jobs contrasts the financial hardships she went through with her mother to the millions earned by her father. It's not clear if Jobs thought he was being cruel or stingy or kind or generous or thoughtful or just thoughtless. He may have been inspired, brilliant and laser-focused when it came to his companies, but he tended to be insensitive when it came to other matters. His daughter was clearly scarred by his actions, financial or otherwise: "For him," Brennan-Jobs wrote in her memoir, "I was a blot on a spectacular ascent, as our story did not fit with the narrative of greatness and virtue he might have wanted of himself. My existence ruined his streak."

John Lennon engendered similar feelings from his son, Julian, born in 1963, just as the Beatles were becoming an international sensation. Although John Lennon provided for his ex-wife and son, it was tough, the younger Lennon said, because others overestimated the financial situation he and his mother found themselves in. "They thought we had millions in the bank," Lennon recalled, "but we never had any money when I was a kid. Mum had enough from Dad for schooling, food and clothes. That was it. Later, the only money I had, I earned." But it wasn't just money, the younger Lennon reflected. It was bewilderment over how a parent, any parent, could ignore a child. "I know bringing up a kid is tough, but I cannot understand how anyone—not just a dad—can walk away from that."

The list of parents facing support requests from lovers and children is tragically long, but for the rich and famous, it is particularly, and perhaps ironically, so. Fabulously rich funnyman Eddie Murphy, a father of ten, denied siring a love child with former Spice Girl Melanie Brown, until a lawsuit—and a paternity test—decided otherwise. English actor and musician Joanne Whalley was forced to take out a lien on an expansive six-thousand-acre ranch in New Mexico owned by her ex-husband, movie star Val Kilmer, when he stopped support payments. Singer Bobby Brown spent a weekend in jail for not paying child support to his children with legendary singer Whitney Houston. Former basketball curiosity Dennis Rodman was convicted of contempt for not paying child support in 2009, and he faced trouble again in 2012 when a judge ordered him to pay his ex $500,000. Many lottery winners seem happy to share their new-found wealth with friends and family, but rich people who feel they've earned their fortune often hug it closer than family.

Despite all those threats, nobody—not the kidnappers, the flim-flammers, the investment schemers, the hapless family members

—is more detested, and more feared, by rich people than a particularly inexorable entity, the likes of which we'll meet in the next chapter: the tax collector.

Trouble and Taxes

Reason No. 7 is that rich people cannot
(or will not) pay their bills.

You might think an inability to pay bills
would make them poor people, not rich
people, but that is not the case. All kinds of
rich people do not pay their bills and somehow still appear rich.
In fact, their refusal to pay their bills may be the reason they are
still rich. Such people include terrifying pugilist Mike Tyson, who
was spending $400,000 a month on high living and overshopping as his career waned and his debts mounted in the late 1990s.
He blew through the $400 million he made during his short and
tempestuous career in the ring and declared bankruptcy in 2003,
owing money to the usual suspects: lawyers, retailers, car dealers,
banks and the Internal Revenue Service. He's not as rich today,
and is perhaps no longer in possession of a treasure chest of jewelry, 110 cars or two hungry Bengal tigers, but he's still somehow
rich, living a "fairly modest" existence, according to a *New York Post*
article, in a ten-thousand-square-foot Las Vegas mansion, despite
the bankruptcy.

Also still rich is Wayne Newton, the lounge singer who gained prominence in the 1960s and is still known today as "Mr. Las Vegas." Famous for songs such as "Danke Schoen," he has been a fixture in Sin City for more than half a century, the highest-grossing entertainer in the city's history. With a partner, he bought the Aladdin casino for $85 million, but declared bankruptcy in 1992, despite earning a reported $250,000 a week as a performer. He had owed money on loans, income taxes, property taxes, lawyers fees, credit cards and storage fees for an airplane that sat dormant in Michigan for years. (Eventually, he settled with the airport and had the plane dismantled and transported to Vegas, where he had it reassembled outside his home.) By the time the new century rolled around, Newton was back on his feet, but he faced new financial woes a decade later, when he was obliged to vacate his beloved estate, known as the Casa de Shenandoah, in 2013, after forty-five years. He ended up in a smaller mansion nearby, which comes with a guest house and four other homes. But according to his sister-in-law, Tricia McCrone, there'd still be enough room for "all his animals—the peacocks, the horses, and Charlie the penguin."

Once upon a time, debtors were forced into slavery or tossed into a dank prison, often without even food or a blanket. They relied on friends and family for sustenance, and they stayed there not until their sentence was served, but until their debts were paid and their creditors satisfied—or until they died. That was the norm for centuries until the 1800s, when much of humanity, led by the United States, came to its senses, and such places were outlawed. And so we now live in an era of bankruptcy laws, not only because they are more humane, or more practical, but because they are considered better for healthy economies.

Modern bankruptcy laws make risk less risky, so entrepreneurs take more chances. The successes, presumably, outweigh the failures. For better and worse, without credit, most of today's economies could not function. It often does not seem fair, but given that standards of living for almost everyone continue to improve, many believe it's the best system available. Others insist there's room for improvement. And as always, the way we discharge debt seems to depend on our wealth, or lack thereof. In her 2009 essay on the history of debtors in the *New Yorker*, Jill Lapore reiterated an age-old reality: "Then, as now, it was better to be rich and owe a fortune than to be poor and owe a pittance."

Such truths have many wondering about the fate of Alex Jones, the ranting conspiracy theorist and volcanic Texas talk-show host who claimed for years that the Sandy Hook school massacre in Connecticut, in which twenty children and six adults died, was a hoax. In 2022, two juries and a judge ordered him to pay almost $1.5 billion to the parents of children killed. Jones immediately declared bankruptcy and announced, "I'm officially out of money."

In reality, he still had at least $2 million by his own reckoning (and $270 million by other estimates), plus four properties, three vehicles and two boats. But perhaps that's as close to penniless as a rich person gets. Regardless of his assets, given the size of the awards, it seems a fair bet that he will indeed be "broke" forever. But it will be a while yet before he's out on the street. Like most rich people, he employs a lot of experts to delay, reduce and avoid his obligations. Texas's Homestead Law, intended to prevent homelessness, will allow Jones to keep at least one of the many luxury homes he bought in the Austin area. And followers and fans have been asked, with some success, for donations.

That kind of thing further enrages those offended by him, partly because Jones's opulent lifestyle was well-documented during his divorce proceedings. In 2014, for example, he bought four Rolex watches in one day. He once spent $40,000 on a saltwater aquarium. At the time, he and his ex-wife owned a $70,000 grand piano,

$50,000 worth of firearms, and $752,000 in silver, gold and other material in a safe deposit box.

And then there were all those homes. Many will want to know what became of such assets—which the *New York Times* revealed have been transferred to family members and friends—and how much he is still spending. Because, like everyone else, he is still spending. Not long after he filed for personal bankruptcy, which resulted in his paycheque being reduced to $20,000 every two weeks, he petitioned the court to reinstate his $1.3 million salary. After all, he still shows up for work every day.

The situation is frustrating the families who won the legal battle but are losing the financial one. The US bankruptcy system prioritizes the survival of businesses, and Jones is being increasingly belligerent about his creditors, abusing and mocking them on his show, and employing every tactic to avoid his obligations. "Without question, Jones is pushing the bankruptcy system to its limits," said Avi Moshenberg, one of the bankruptcy lawyers representing the families.

For all the good things that bankruptcy laws and credit arrangements have delivered to modern society, another darker side is the inexorable rise in personal debt, fuelled by banks and institutions that encourage us all to buy now and pay later. Household debt continues to increase in Canada, the United States, Europe and beyond, reaching record highs in 2022, even without mortgage loans. Shopping without money, buying stuff without funds and using plastic for all purchases has become a way of life for many people, encouraged by voracious credit-card companies that prey on consumers. It's a problem for the rich and poor alike.

It was an initial challenge for Toni Braxton. Famous as the singer of "Un-Break My Heart," Braxton was once labelled "the poster child of Hollywood's wild rollercoaster—flying high, falling down and then bouncing back." She's now been bankrupt twice; her first the result of an addiction to housewares: "I love dishes and house things, so I kind of lost it a little bit." The second was due to illness during a self-financed Las Vegas show. More open than most about her financial troubles, Braxton told the world on her reality TV show, *Braxton Family Values*, that she made the best of it, and was thrilled after she won an order discharging her from some debts. (The court had earlier approved a deal permitting her to keep various treasured household goods, jewelry, a piano and a Porsche.) "My bankruptcy situation worked out really great for me."

That probably isn't the way other celebrities would describe it. For most, it is nothing less than an ordeal. In 2015, the reality star, model and philanthropist Sonja Morgan declared bankruptcy when she was unable to pay debts of more than $19 million. The star of *The Real Housewives of New York City* and the ex-wife of J.P. Morgan heir John Morgan settled the case after five years and said she was relieved, finally, to have her "financial privacy" back: "It's nice to be free of everyone looking at my money." She also managed to keep her home in Manhattan, which has been for sale, on and off, during the last decade for between $7 million and $10 million: "I'm keeping the townhouse," she said at the time. "I let the Colorado house go and I sold the house in France."

More recently, reality TV stars Todd and Julie Chrisley went to jail in 2023 for conspiring to defraud banks and evading taxes. Famous for the show *Chrisley Knows Best*, they portrayed themselves as hard-working real estate moguls with high-living tastes. The millions they made on television weren't enough to support the illusion, however, and to maintain it they did not pay taxes from 2013 to 2016, filing false statements and hiding income from tax collectors. Further, they acquired $36 million in personal loans from banks in Atlanta by submitting fake statements and documents.

After they were convicted, prosecutors summed up the scam: "The Chrisleys have built an empire based on the lie that their wealth came from dedication and hard work. The jury's unanimous verdict sets the record straight: Todd and Julie Chrisley are career swindlers who have made a living by jumping from one fraud scheme to another, lying to banks, stiffing vendors and evading taxes at every corner." If they serve their full sentences, Julie will be released by 2030 and Todd in 2035. Both maintain their innocence.

Another former bankrupt who is famously still rich is the musician, actor and business executive Curtis Jackson, sometimes known as the rapper 50 Cent. A former drug dealer who survived being shot nine times, he filed for bankruptcy in 2015 (the year *Forbes* estimated his net worth at $155 million) to erase debts after overshopping, bad investments and legal problems. In 2020, however, he posed for photos on Instagram with stacks of cash. Jackson explained the situation to a judge: "Just because I am photographed in or next to a certain vehicle, wearing an article of clothing, holding a product, sitting next to what appears to be large sums of money or modeling expensive pieces of jewelry does not mean that I own everything in those photos."

Yes, appearances can be deceiving, especially when it comes to rich people. Boris Becker, a German national hero and former tennis champion, once fancied himself the master of illusion to avoid financial obligations. The man that media dubbed "Boom Boom Boris" spent almost as much time trying to avoid paying his bills as he did nurturing a tennis career, during which he earned what he told a judge was a "vast amount," estimated at more than $170 million. After retirement in 1999, he published an autobiography, took up professional poker playing and became a tennis coach.

But his financial troubles were evident by 2002, when he had officially and ostensibly moved to Monaco, where he could avoid taxes. In fact, however, he had not moved at all, and instead spent most of his time holed up in an apartment in Germany, where he was obliged to pay them. Authorities were unimpressed. He paid the taxes owed, but they fined him 300,000 euros and gave him a two-year suspended sentence. By that time, his marriage had fallen apart, the result, perhaps, of a notorious tryst with a Russian model in the broom closet of a fancy London restaurant (which produced a daughter). "The most expensive five seconds of my life," Becker would famously recall, finally admitting the girl was his, and agreeing to a £2 million lump sum and £25,000 a month in payments to his paramour. His wife, who was pregnant at the time, would eventually get a £15-million settlement and custody of their children (see Reason No. 6). And the entire mess was splashed endlessly on the front pages of tabloid newspapers and beyond (see Reason No. 1).

By 2017, unable to make the payments on his luxury estate in Mallorca, Spain, Becker was forced into bankruptcy proceedings, owing nearly £50 million. Before his possessions could be auctioned off to pay creditors, he claimed to have been appointed a sporting, cultural and humanitarian attaché to the Central African Republic, and therefore had diplomatic immunity against legal action. The Central African Republic denied any knowledge of such an arrangement. In 2022, Becker went to jail after a jury found him guilty of hiding his assets from creditors. The judge in the case said Becker showed no remorse and accepted no guilt: "While I accept your humiliation as part of the proceedings, there has been no humility."

Indeed, humility is sometimes difficult to find among the rich. Patricia Kluge, who took a philosophical approach to her own financial disaster, may be an exception. She grew up in Baghdad, but at age twenty-seven, she met John Kluge after performing a belly dance at a party in Manhattan. In 1981, she married the sixty-two-year-old billionaire, moved into a palatial mansion in Virginia called Albemarle and entertained the rich and powerful at elegant soirees and weekend hunting parties. After her divorce in 1990, she was said to be worth more than $100 million, much of which she plowed into an elegant and respected winery she developed at her estate. By 2011, however, the operation had proven more challenging than she had expected, and she declared bankruptcy, forced to sell the winery and the beloved estate itself to Donald Trump. But she seemed to take it all in stride. "I loved life at Albemarle, are you kidding?" she later told the *New York Times*. "But it does not define who I am. No one should feel sorry for us."

As humans, we all like spending money. Some more than others. But as much as we enjoy it, nobody, even extravagant wastrels, wants to spend more than we have to. Rich people may seem like spendthrifts, but they are just like the rest of us. Even if they are not concerned about going bankrupt or running out of money, everyone wants a bargain. Nobody wants to pay full price. It doesn't matter if we are buying caviar at a specialty shop or a hamburger at the drive-thru. We want a deal, which may be why every store in the mall seems permanently rife with announcements of alleged "sales." We haggle with car dealers or real estate agents or the market vendor.

Often, this is expected of us; and sometimes, if we're rich, it just looks cheap. Worse, while doing it before a transaction may be one thing, doing it after the sale is an option for some rich people. They want to buy, but they don't want to pay. There may be no one more famous in this category than the twice-impeached president of the United States, Donald Trump.

Long a poster child for stinginess, he was the subject of an exhaustive 2016 examination by US A *Today* that indicated he has been involved in legal disputes with painters, lawyers, cabinet makers, a plumber, a dishwasher, bartenders, waiters, contractors, realtors and various other workers over the years. Trump once explained he didn't pay these lowly stiffs because their work was substandard. "Let's say that they do a job that's not good, or a job that they didn't finish, or a job that was way late. I'll delete that from their contract, absolutely."

A lot of poor people, or even moderately rich people, might well wonder whether Trump did any due diligence before hiring these people. Yet, inexplicably, he was known to occasionally rehire for new jobs the same folks he refused to pay for old jobs (see Reason No. 2). His businesses, meanwhile, were singled out over a ten-year period between 2005 and 2015 for various violations of the Fair Labor Standards Act. "I fight like hell to pay as little as possible," Trump once boasted. And in another interview, he indicated why: "I know when I'm being overcharged. Other people don't and they're suckers."

To be sure, nobody likes being a sucker, but it seems to be a particular fear among rich people, especially penny-pinchers with big egos. In Trump's case, he goes out of his way to declare every business venture, no matter how disastrous, a tremendous victory. His ill-fated sojourn in three Atlantic City casinos, which lost money and went bankrupt in the 1990s, is a good example. Those were tough days for the self-promoting developer: lenders forced him to sell his airline and his yacht, among other things, and put him on an allowance of just $450,000 a month for personal and household expenses. He had borrowed so heavily and at such high interest rates, the casinos collapsed under the weight of all that debt, leaving bond holders, investors and small businesses in the lurch. For Trump, though, things ultimately turned out well, and he judged the experience a bonanza: "Atlantic City fueled a lot of growth for me," Trump once told the *New York Times*. "The money I took out of there was incredible."

Famously delinquent and tyrannical hotelier Leona Helmsley was another business executive who hated to pay for services. Her alleged refusal to pay contractors at her Connecticut home led to one of the highest-profile trials of the 1980s. Famous today for the statement "Only little people pay taxes," Helmsley faced federal income tax evasion charges, amid other crimes, including extortion, all because she refused to pay contractors. She and her husband had a fortune exceeding $1 billion, but they were famously reluctant to settle up with mere workers making extravagant improvements to their weekend place, a twenty-one-room mansion in Connecticut.

When the contractors sued, it emerged that their work was being illegally billed to the Helmsleys' hotel business, and the feds arrived to investigate. "Nothing was too small or personal to be billed to their businesses," wrote the *New York Times* in her obituary, "from Mrs. Helmsley's bras to a white lace and pink satin dress and jacket and a white chiffon skirt—the dress and skirt were entered in the Park Lane Hotel records as uniforms for the staff." Helmsley went to jail and spent her years after prison mostly alone in her penthouse atop New York's Park Lane Hotel. Her will left a $12-million trust fund to her dog, Trouble, but nothing to two of her grandchildren.

Governments and law enforcement officials are not always so successful at prosecuting rich people they allege had their hands in the till. Since 2017, for example, the Indian government has been trying to extradite Vijay Mallya, a billionaire liquor baron once known as the "King of Good Times." A former member of India's parliament, he once owned a cricket franchise, a Formula 1 racing team and an ill-fated airline, but he departed India for Britain in 2016 as his money troubles mounted and authorities closed in. He has never returned. Among his various unpaid bills was $1 million in back pay owed to the crew of his superyacht, the *Indian Empress*. A Maltese court ordered the vessel to be sold to pay creditors, including the crew, but the Indian government has been less successful in seeking justice. By 2023, Mallya was still on bail, living a life of relative luxury in England.

Carlos Ghosn, former head of both Renault and Nissan, is also on the lam for money allegedly owed. Born in Brazil and a citizen of France, Ghosn is wanted by Interpol for misappropriating funds while leading both car companies. Once seen as a hard-working, accomplished business magician, he saw his status unravel in 2018, when Nissan alleged he had misappropriated company money and Japanese authorities arrested him. In 2019, while on bail, he secreted himself in an audio equipment box that was smuggled out of Japan by a US Army Special Forces veteran and his son. Today, he lives in Beirut, insisting on his innocence and alleging the Japanese justice system is "rigged." While Ghosn continues to burnish his reputation with the help of a Hollywood agent, Nissan has locked his family members out of apartments in Rio and Paris allegedly bought with company funds, and the father-son team who helped him escape went to jail.

The tradition of rich people behaving imperiously in business goes back thousands of years. The so-called robber barons, a term coined in America in the nineteenth century to describe the likes of John Jacob Astor or Cornelius Vanderbilt, were particularly adept. These men would do anything to avoid paying more than required, and would pay even less if they could. The monopolists were widely thought to engage in unethical practices and abuse workers, investors and customers alike.

Vanderbilt, one of the richest individuals in American history, was a ruthless operator, a stock manipulator and a nasty misogynist. He cut wages indiscriminately, among various other trespasses against his workers, but was nonetheless considered a better employer than some.

In his book *John Jacob Astor: America's First Multimillionaire*, Axel Madsen describes the German-born entrepreneur, who initially made his money in the fur trade, as "also a slumlord, a war profiteer, and a ruthless jobber who shipped opium to China, and sold liquor to Indians knowing the devastating consequences." The movers and shakers of the Gilded Age exploited natural resources, abused workers, ignored safety precautions, bribed government officials and amassed wealth without thought to those less fortunate. And still some observers and historians remember them fondly as captains of early industry.

Today, 150 years later, the formula for success isn't much different: pay as little as possible while charging as much as possible. The rich owners of Starbucks and Amazon, to name only a few high-profile companies, have the same mixed reputations. Are Howard Schultz and Jeff Bezos to be praised for revolutionizing coffee culture and home delivery, and, indeed, for changing the world? Are they to be congratulated for hiring all those employees, admired for contributing to a healthy economy, and thanked for giving away millions of dollars? Or criticized for anti-union tactics and exploitation of workers, for the destruction of family businesses, and for various environmental trespasses?

It is a cliché that rich entrepreneurs didn't get that way without stepping on a lot of toes, and in a world where today's captains of industry have so much when others have so little, they will always face criticism that they didn't pay their fair share—of bills, of wages, of benefits, of environmental restoration costs, of municipal infrastructure fees, but especially (and persistently) of taxes.

Nobody likes giving money to governments. They seem to ding us at every opportunity and spend our money with abandon on projects few can agree on. But most of us accept taxes as a necessary evil, our civic duty, or the price of a reasonably functioning society. Many rich people feel differently, and often think they know better how such monies should be spent. For them, taxes are problems that must be eliminated. And with so much money at their disposal, they've found myriad ways to circumvent them. They may not want to pony up for the tax collector, but they have no issues throwing money at scheming tax experts, creative accountants and clever lawyers to avoid paying even one cent more than is necessary.

Real estate is a favourite tax haven often not available to lesser beings. Some buy racehorses or hotels that may lose money. And then there are sports teams. More than ten per cent of people on the *Forbes* 400 list own sports teams, most of which demand that taxpayers shell out billions for stadiums, arenas and other venues to attract people who aren't quite as rich to pay hundreds of dollars to attend events, drink beer, eat hot dogs and buy merch.

In his book *Free Lunch: How the Wealthiest Americans Enrich Themselves at Government Expense (and Stick You with the Bill)*, David Cay Johnston says dozens of billionaires own sports teams that require government assistance, and leagues restrict who can buy a team and where it can play. It is, he says, one of the "great ironies of our time. Commercial sports games are about competition, but the leagues themselves are exempt from the laws of competition."

The rich bully governments for sweet deals. They battle tax collectors in court. They hide their money in offshore banks. They move to places like Monaco or the Bahamas.

In particularly inept cases, they simply ignore the tax bill, like country crooner Willie Nelson, or action star Wesley Snipes—until it becomes a problem. Nelson received a bill for $16.7 million in back taxes in 1990, and cut the album *The IRS Tapes: Who'll Buy My Memories?* to help satisfy the government. Snipes went to jail in 2010 for disregarding a $7 million bill, and upon his release more than two years later, reflected on the experience: "The biggest thing I got from it was learning the value of time and how we often squander it," he said, admitting he was "not an innocent bystander" in the debacle, but emerged "clearer on what I was going to do once I had my freedom back." Tarnished baseball great Pete Rose, pioneering rock 'n' roller Chuck Berry and iconic Italian movie star Sophia Loren all spent time in jail for not paying their taxes. (A court in

Rome admitted it erred in the case of Loren—three decades after she served her sentence.)

Sometimes, rich people move to a place where such tax annoyances simply don't exist. For former Bond movie actors Roger Moore and Sean Connery, that meant being labelled tax dodgers, much to their chagrin. Moore, who had homes in Switzerland and Monaco, and Connery, who had a place in the Bahamas and another in Spain, were dogged by accusations they abandoned their beloved native lands for places they could live in the manner to which they'd become accustomed. Both vehemently denied the charges. Phil Collins said he moved to Switzerland for love; Formula 1 racing star Lewis Hamilton, convicted for reckless driving on public roads, said he moved there for privacy. Both excuses seem reasonable, but both men still get labelled tax exiles. It's easy to imagine that many tax exiles were not inconvenienced at home; they simply enjoy the climate, the architecture, the food or the people in exotic locales, with lower taxes as a fringe benefit.

But many such moves are financially motivated. When Mick Jagger and the Rolling Stones moved to France in 1971, it was common knowledge they did it to avoid a heftier tax bill. Ironically, as their wealth grew, they said they couldn't afford to live in Britain. Abandoning rainy England, they decamped to various luxury villas along France's sunny Côte d'Azur, cutting the now-classic *Exile on Main St.* album in the basement of Keith Richards's villa. Jagger and Richards remain tax exiles to this day. Arranging such accommodations, let alone the moving expenses, may be a problem for rich people, but it's an impossibility for poorer people, who simply cannot afford such freedoms; they're stuck at home paying taxes or going to jail.

Many rich people stay happily at home yet ship their money elsewhere. They have tricks for hiding, shielding and delaying income to ease their tax burden, creating complex financial apparatuses that are somehow legal, and if not, often go undiscovered.

These business constructs are often so opaque and impenetrable even their legitimate heirs cannot unravel them without help from expensive lawyers and accountants.

The matter of "accommodating jurisdictions"—nations where it is easy to park money—is one of the most tenacious challenges for cash-strapped governments around the world. For the last several hundred years, most people kept their cash at the local bank, where they walked in weekly to make deposits or withdrawals and received a (very) modest interest payment regularly. Richer people put spare cash in bonds or the stock markets with help from brokers and advisors. Some invest in real estate, gold, art or perhaps a friend or family member's business, if they're feeling brave.

But the superrich have all that and offshore accounts too. Switzerland, Luxembourg, the British Virgin Islands, Bermuda, the Cayman Islands and Panama, among many others, are tax havens for the very rich. There, lawyers, accountants and other expensive helpers set up shell companies to move money around or just park it quietly for a rainy day. Sometimes these companies are created solely to take ownership of assets such as art or real estate.

These accounts are not necessarily illegal. Sometimes these clients simply like the sound of having a Swiss bank account. Or, like so many rich people, they're paranoid about losing their fortune. Or maybe they appreciate the famously stable European country and the renowned efficiency and discretion of its residents. Maybe they like tropical islands or maybe they like to keep money in more than one piggy bank.

But mostly they want to keep their fortune from prying eyes. The two biggest reasons for such accounts are protection of assets and privacy. These operations, writes Alain Deneault in his book *Legalizing Theft: A Short Guide to Tax Havens,* allow rich people "to escape the control of state institutions and carry out speculative operations that have no actual economic relevance." In Canada, he adds, they benefit from public infrastructure and services largely funded by the middle class.

We all knew these accounts existed. They are the stuff of spy novels and Mafia movies. But they are multiplying as fast as, well, rich people. By some accounts, the amount being moved into offshore accounts from home countries nearly doubled to almost $1 trillion worldwide between 2015 and 2019. Ironically, that followed a coordinated effort by the world's biggest economies to battle the trend.

As helpless as governments have been to stanch the bleeding, journalists and others have been working hard to expose it. In 2016, following a series of widely publicized data leaks to the International Consortium of Investigative Journalists (ICIJ), a group of hundreds of journalists around the world, the public got a better picture of just how widespread the practice is. When the so-called Panama Papers were released in 2016, followed by the Paradise Papers in 2017 and the Pandora Papers in 2021, reporters exposed millions of confidential documents revealing who, when, where and how the rich use offshore accounts.

The "why" often remains unspoken, but the Pandora Papers revealed that international tax avoidance efforts are a key reason for offshore accounts. Trillions of dollars are said to be in these accounts, untaxed and unrecorded, around the world. Most of these places have several things in common: extremely low tax rates, permissive legal systems, authorities who don't pry, famously secretive banks and businesses that don't actually do anything except shuffle money around.

These operations can be legitimate vehicles for the rich, or shady spots for criminals to hide and launder money. Celebrities may want to make real estate purchases or buy a yacht without the sellers knowing who's ponying up the money. According to the Pandora Papers, Elton John has a dozen companies in the British Virgin

Islands, and Julio Iglesias owns more than twenty companies there. Other account holders may want to protect assets from potential creditors (you just never know when you're going to be sued, or by whom) or avoid public scrutiny. Many are mysteriously controlled by suspiciously rich dictators who know that when judgment day comes, their ill-gotten gains will not be safe in a hometown bank.

Hun Sen, the ensconced leader of Cambodia since 1985, who has presided over years of corruption and cronyism, not to mention human rights violations and an astonishing rate of deforestation, may share a fortune of $1 billion with family members. A Reuters investigation in 2019 indicated many of them—as well as police, business and political associates—are keeping their fortunes offshore, creating an elaborate escape plan for the inevitable day when everything goes south, and purchasing foreign citizenships.

The leader himself has condemned such "purchases," but he's well aware, like any student of history, that secret funds can be needed in a hurry. There is simmering discontent in Cambodia; it's only a matter of time before his rule ends. "Everyone is making an escape plan," according to one government official quoted by Reuters.

Abdullah II, the king of Jordan, clearly isn't using offshore accounts to avoid taxes. He's the king, after all, and doesn't pay them anyway. But the sixty-year-old monarch does have an image to maintain. In 2020, following popular uprisings, Jordan announced a crackdown on rich people who hide money and own offshore accounts. Too much cash, apparently, was flowing out of the country, and it had to be stopped. What was not clear at the time was that the king himself secretly owned fourteen luxury homes abroad, according to the ICIJ. Purchased between 2003 and 2017 in the United States and England, they are valued at more than $100 million: three adjoining beachfront homes in Los Angeles, plus a mansion overlooking the ocean; luxury apartments in Washington and central London; a house in the English countryside.

The king has more than just an image to maintain; he has a restless population to keep docile, and news like this would not help him with his compatriots, let alone foreign governments that throw billions in foreign aid at Jordan. "The Pandora Papers investigation reveals that Abdullah has owned at least 36 front companies in secret tax havens," writes Will Fitzgibbon of the ICIJ. "Email exchanges found among the leaked files show that for Abdullah's financial advisers, concealing the king's links to the companies, and the properties they acquired, was Job One."

None of us really wants to share financial information with others, but rich people are particularly reluctant to open their books. In 2021, ProPublica, a non-profit newsroom that investigates abuses of power, acquired a trove of IRS tax return data on thousands of rich people in the United States over more than a decade, and began pointing a spotlight at the lengths to which rich people go to avoid paying their fair share. The team's conclusions: many ultrarich Americans are able to entirely sidestep the income tax system. While mere millionaires are dinged pretty hard, some American billionaires paid no taxes in some years, mostly because only wages and salaries are taxed, not the growth of their capital holdings. For that reason and others, the "true tax rate" those billionaires pay, according to ProPublica, is a mere fraction of the average working Joe.

As an example of how billionaires use the system to their advantage, ProPublica pointed to Peter Thiel, the US billionaire and founder of PayPal. Famous for his opposition to what he called "confiscatory taxes," Thiel once invested $1.7 million in the Seasteading Institute, which hoped to build a huge, nationless, floating libertarian paradise, a Shangri-La free from the traditional politics, economics and rules that burden modern democracies, before bowing out of the project and admitting it wouldn't work.

But maybe he didn't need it after all. According to ProPublica, Thiel uses a US retirement-savings vehicle called a Roth IRA, designed for middle-class Americans, that will allow him to avoid $5 billion in taxes. If he doesn't withdraw any money until age fifty-nine, he doesn't pay a dime. Ted Weschler, who works with Warren Buffett at Berkshire Hathaway, had $264.4 million in his Roth account at the end of 2018. When ProPublica reached him for a comment, he admitted he was a beneficiary of the system but did not think it was "necessarily good tax policy."

In 2018, the unpredictable industrialist Elon Musk, at the time the richest man in the world, paid no US income tax. Amazon founder Jeff Bezos paid none in 2011. This kind of feat is achieved regularly by the richest of the rich, mostly because the US system taxes wages and salaries, not necessarily income from capital investments.

Donald Trump often boasts about winning, but a *New York Times* investigation revealed he paid no income tax in eleven of eighteen years due to business losses, and only $750 in each of 2016 and 2017, his first two years as president. (His presidential successor, Joe Biden, and his wife paid $150,439 in income tax 2021 and $137,658 in 2022.) Ron Wyden, a US senator helping lead the fight to make the rich pay more taxes, says the system as it is "causes people to lose faith in government, lose faith in democracy."

Others find high taxes such a problem that they are willing to invest millions to lobby governments—and the people—to keep them low. In 2020, Ken Griffin, a hedge-fund founder and the richest man in Illinois, spent $54 million on advertising and other efforts in that state to fight a proposal on the ballot to raise taxes for the wealthy. It worked: voters deep-sixed the proposal.

Sure, the $54 million seems an outrageous expense, but according to ProPublica, it may have saved Griffin, who earned an average annual income of $1.7 billion from 2013 to 2018, as much as $80 million in a single year. So even without the payback, it was, relatively speaking, a drop in the bucket. After all, Griffin, an art collector, once spent half a billion dollars on only two paintings in what *Bloomberg News* called "one of the largest private art deals ever." He told ProPublica he's not against taxes, just that particular measure: "Illinois needs to put its fiscal house in order before burdening hard-working families with more taxes."

Many politicians agree. They believe people lose faith in government because taxes are too high. Many government services are unnecessary, they argue, and the private sector is better suited to solving social ills. Not surprisingly, they are easily swayed by rich people, and some are rich themselves. Donald Trump and former New York mayor Michael Bloomberg are billionaires. US Senator Mitt Romney, a Republican, and former US senator John Kerry, a Democrat, may have $200 million each. Canadian Prime Minister Justin Trudeau has millions; so does former Canadian prime minister Paul Martin. Britain's Prime Minister Rishi Sunak has a billion. Russian leader Vladimir Putin may have more than $100 billion, despite a salary of $140,000.

Some politicians want to raise taxes on the rich, but most campaign on a promise to lower taxes, especially for the wealthy— efforts that are often remarkably successful. They are influenced by rich people, some who simply don't want to pay and threaten to let them know at the voting booth. Elizabeth Warren, once a Democratic candidate for president of the United States, summed up the situation for a CNBC interviewer during her 2019 campaign: "Government listens disproportionately to rich guys who don't want to pay taxes."

Among the more prominent such puppeteers are the secretive Koch brothers, Charles and his late brother David, US industrialists who have given more than $100 million to conservative and libertarian groups in the United States. Involved in a vast array of philanthropic interests from medicine to museums to the arts, they are perhaps better known for funding and organizing groups that push for lower taxes, deregulation and small government.

The Koch brothers had always been combative. Charles and David won a nasty and protracted battle against their brothers, Fred and Bill, for control of Koch Industries that lasted through the 1980s and '90s. While they had always been active in conservative political circles, they ramped up their activities after Barack Obama was elected president of the United States, as Jane Mayer outlines in her book *Dark Money*.

After the financial crisis of 2008 and the ensuing economic devastation, it may have seemed eminently reasonable to the newly elected US president to say during his first inaugural address that "the nation cannot prosper when it favors only the prosperous" and that "a free market only thrives when there are rules to ensure competition and fair play." He added that the economy had been weakened because of "greed and irresponsibility" and that "without a watchful eye, the market can spin out of control." He repeated many of these themes upon re-election four years later.

Opponents like the Kochs, however, heard a war cry against business, free enterprise and the almighty power of the markets to solve the ills of society. Long supporters of the Libertarian Party (Charles spent $2 million to run for president under the banner in 1980), they believed it presaged economic disaster and would lead down a road to ruin for America's rich.

Their solution was to bankroll a variety of organizations, think tanks and publications to push back against anything that Obama favoured. They spent hundreds of millions to assemble a new and powerful lobby of those committed to free enterprise, fewer restrictions on business and free reign for billionaires. These groups include Americans for Prosperity, the Heritage Foundation and the Manhattan Institute, which oppose clean energy and carbon legislation and anything that might inconvenience private enterprise.

Even with the devastation of the financial crisis still fresh in their collective memories, half the population bought in. The effort helped spawn the Tea Party in the United States and similar sentiments beyond its borders. And it culminated, perhaps, in the MAGA universe, where Donald Trump became an international darling of those who think government—and taxes—are a problem.

The Koch brothers are notoriously averse to publicity, but in 2011, after fellow billionaire Warren Buffett wrote in the *New York Times* that "while most Americans struggle to make ends meet, we mega-rich continue to get our extraordinary tax breaks," Charles Koch could not stay quiet: "I believe my business and non-profit investments are much more beneficial to societal well-being than sending more money to Washington."

That kind of thinking goes back to Adam Smith, author of *The Wealth of Nations*, who believed unfettered capitalism would benefit all society: "By pursuing his own interest, he frequently promotes that of the society more effectually than when he really intends to promote it. I have never known much good done by those who affected trade for the public good." The theory, more or less, has guided rich people ever since: leave business people alone to make money and the money will trickle down.

What is overlooked is that without a functioning government, tariffs, trade agreements and often subsidies for businesses, such profits are impossible. And without enough taxes, governments don't function. And without functioning governments, most rich people would be poorer. Beyond that, many rich people abuse the systems they criticize, presiding over monumental business failures or looting their own companies, shareholders and employees in pursuit of more for themselves.

Affluence and Anxiety

*"The billionaire bashing needs to happen.
I don't know why we're being so polite."*

—Abigail Disney, multimillionaire

Reason No. 8 is that nobody seems to like rich people.

Ironically, lots of rich people are quite nice. As a matter of fact (if you'll pardon the cliché), some of my best friends, acquaintances and family members are rich, and they are very nice indeed. They seem genuinely kind, not just to friends but also to strangers. They give to charity, they help people, they care about the world around them, and while they live well, they don't live ostentatiously, notwithstanding the fact it's tempting to when you have so much. But these are not the type most of us think of when we contemplate the wealthy. Looking for foibles, failings and faults is more popular, and more fun.

Some of us are envious of wealth and fame. Others, given the excess often displayed by the superrich, simply can't resist marvelling at the many ways that rich people create problems for themselves through their own extravagance. A case in point: Amazon founder Jeff Bezos generated negative headlines worldwide in 2022 when building his new half-a-billion-dollar yacht in Rotterdam. The shipyard wanted permission to remove part of a historic bridge to allow it to sail out to sea, but the request caused such a backlash locally they scrapped the plan and towed the yacht to another yard to be completed. No expense was spared, and the builders thought of almost everything—except how to get it quietly out to sea.

Some feel that many rich people have not played fair: they lie and cheat and scheme and do not deserve all that cash. Most bankers who helped plunge the world into the economic crisis of 2008 did not face any legal consequences, and many are still super-rich. Some conniving chief executives have gone to jail, deservedly, but the general public can't shake the feeling that too many others continue their illegal deeds with impunity. Sports icons such as baseball slugger Alex Rodriguez and cyclist Lance Armstrong are still fabulously rich despite admitting they cheated their way to huge paycheques. Paul Manafort, a Washington lobbyist and lawyer famous for being Donald Trump's campaign chair in 2016, is still rich, despite having been tried, convicted and jailed for laundering money, among various other charges related to his opaque operations with foreign governments. Trump later pardoned him.

Chronicling the problems of the rich is a kind of deranged sport for the masses and a gleeful career for television producers, filmmakers and writers like me. *Dallas* and *Dynasty* defined rich people for a generation of TV watchers in the 1980s. *Yellowstone* and *Succession* and *The White Lotus* are streaming sensations today. *The Wolf of Wall Street*, *Parasite* and *Triangle of Sadness*, among dozens, perhaps hundreds, of other movies, are somehow both compelling and appalling. It's a love-hate relationship. We want what rich people have, but we don't want their problems, and just knowing they are miserable can make us feel better.

Abigail Disney, the granddaughter of Roy Disney, co-founder of the Walt Disney Company, believes the animosity toward rich people is not only warranted but necessary. She is among a growing number of rich people who don't think much of rich people, particularly billionaires. A multimillionaire herself, she believes too much money is as bad for individuals as it is for society. Riding in a private jet, she once said, "hollows you out from the inside."

Disney is frank about her own rich lifestyle: the benefits, including eating at the best restaurants and drinking expensive wine; and the drawbacks, including not feeling legitimate and struggling to find friends who can see beyond all that cash. Disney, who made a documentary film, *The American Dream and Other Fairy Tales*, calling out the Disney company for pay inequality, could easily have become a billionaire rather than a mere multimillionaire, she says, because once you have a lot, it's very easy to make lots more. She says she has already given away more than she inherited, and still has plenty.

In her opinion, millionaires are spendthrifts and polluters, and rich corporate owners should be trying harder to decarbonize, to uphold feminist principles and to guarantee a living wage for employees, among other things. Governments should be taxing them more. "Billionaires are miserable, unhappy people. The billionaire bashing needs to happen. I don't know why we're being so polite."

Elizabeth Koch, daughter of the controversial billionaire industrialist Charles Koch, recently told an interviewer she has dedicated her life to a single pursuit: "To not be hated."

It is no secret that rich people are not like everyone else. But is the hostility toward them deserved? The research of Paul Piff, an associate professor of psychological science at the University of California, Berkeley, suggests this animosity toward the rich may be a result of their own actions. Rich people, in his experiments at least, seem less concerned about the welfare of others.

In a funny-not-funny TED talk (it has had three million views on YouTube), Piff outlines some of the now-famous experiments that have led him and his team to believe this. One involves a rigged Monopoly game. Two players flip a coin. The winner is given more money to start and gets $200 when he passes Go; the loser gets half as much money and only $100 when he passes Go. The former gets two dice, the latter only one. Predictably, the rich players get richer. And they immediately begin behaving less charitably toward the poor player. What's more, after the experiment, says Piff, "when the rich players talked about why they'd inevitably won in this rigged game of Monopoly, they talked about what *they'd* done to buy those different properties and earn their success in the game."

Another experiment involved observing the kinds of cars that stopped for a pedestrian at a crosswalk. Some drove blithely through the intersection, breaking the law, and others stopped and waited patiently for the pedestrian to cross. Guess which ones did what? "None of the cars, *none* of the cars, in our least expensive car category, broke the law," said Piff. "Close to 50 per cent of the cars in our most expensive category broke the law."

When it was released a decade ago, the study generated a lot of headlines, buzz and, mostly from rich people, outrage. And why not? It demonstrated that rich people were more likely to lie when negotiating, cheat to help themselves win and "take valued goods from others" than poorer people. Other studies by Piff and his team indicate that "social class is associated with increased entitlement and narcissism." Economic inequality isn't just bad for those at the bottom, he says, but for society itself.

He is quick to add, though, that all is not lost, because rich people are not completely incorrigible. In other experiments, Piff exposed rich people to the challenges facing poor people, having them watch videos on child poverty, for example, and they immediately softened. The problem is that rich people tend to insulate themselves from such unpleasantness. They buy homes in gated communities and winter residences in expensive ski resorts. They vacation on imposing yachts or private islands. They travel by private jet or limousine, shop in exclusive stores and eat in the best restaurants, so for most of their lives they are surrounded by other rich people (see Reason No. 3).

Not only does isolation make rich people's problems seem bigger than they are, because they are comparing themselves with other rich people, but they tend to (or try to) forget the teeming masses of starving children and the unwashed poor just beyond the gates. The really rich erect barriers, and the moderately rich move to neighbourhoods or cities where the nasty consequences of urbanization and gentrification (among other things) are hidden from sight. Says Piff: "Wealth buys us space from other people."

It's not something many care to admit. In the 2020 documentary *Created Equal*, US Supreme Court Justice Clarence Thomas said he favoured vacationing at "RV parks. I prefer the Walmart parking lots to the beaches and things like that. There's something normal to me about it. I come from regular stock, and I prefer that—I prefer being around that." While that may be his stated preference, the reality is often more upscale, according to a 2023 investigation by ProPublica. What Thomas didn't say—and didn't report—was that he and his wife have been regular holiday guests of Republican mega-donor Harlan Crow, travelling on his jet, touring such places as Indonesia on Crow's superyacht, joining Crow at exclusive retreats and spending a week every summer at Topridge, Crow's private resort in upper New York State's Adirondack Mountains. Such exclusive destinations are not the kind of places where one normally finds "regular stock."

Not all rich people are the same, of course. In fact, a surprising number of rich people, especially those who have been rich for some time, try to avoid conspicuous consumption, although that is certainly open to interpretation. And there seem to be many who are at least marginally aware of the world around them and feel at least slightly guilty about their fortunate lot in life, according to Rachel Sherman, who studied fifty affluent New Yorkers for her book *Uneasy Street: The Anxieties of Affluence*.

The people Sherman featured worried about their own consumerism and wastefulness, how it affected the environment, and how others perceived their tastes in the finer things in life. They felt guilty about not having to work, or not having to worry about paying the rent. They worried about how to raise children who would not be spoiled or feel entitled. Their problem was money itself. While they appreciated all that cash, they agonized about its effects. They were conflicted, writes Sherman: "the vast majority implicitly or explicitly indicated that they had some kind of moral concern about having wealth."

Those are not the kinds of problems most of us normally equate with the rich. Concerns like that don't come naturally to the wealthy, and as Sherman points out, those who are aware tend to justify their consumerism and their wealthy existence as they age. "Even those who have been most uncomfortable with affluent lifestyles grow accustomed to their advantages," she writes. They buy more stuff, hire more people, live more expensively, either without recognizing the changes or simply justifying them as necessary, beneficial or inevitable.

As Piff demonstrated, many rich people reach out naturally to help because they are exposed to those in need. But others are philanthropic because they are expected to be. Some give because they want to be admitted into social circles where such behaviour is *de rigueur*. We all want to be remembered favourably in obituaries. Many humanitarians are sincere, but others are trying to assuage critics, remind the world that they aren't as evil as advertised, or simply counter the growing impression that people don't like them very much.

Almost all of them believe they are doing some good, but some believe they alone can fix societal ills that others, especially governments, cannot, and they throw their money at problems to demonstrate their power or know-how. Whether or not they are justified, rich people tend to believe they are smarter than almost everyone else. Maybe it's because they're told as much so often, or maybe because they truly believe their superior intellect, work ethic and intelligence earned them their money.

But while humans as a species have proven over millennia that we tend to do what we're told, as individuals we don't like it much. And we especially don't like rich know-it-alls. They can't seem to resist telling others how to run their lives, and that means a life of politics, either as backroom influencers and puppeteers like billionaire financier George Soros or billionaire industrialist Charles Koch, or actual practitioners, like the former Italian prime minister Silvio Berlusconi or the former US president Donald Trump. And that means increased scrutiny from media and a growing number of haters.

Soros has donated more than $30 billion to various causes, which *Forbes* magazine said in 2021 qualified him as the world's "most generous giver" when measured as a percentage of his net worth. A Hungarian by birth, he moved to Britain and then to the United States as a young man and made a fortune in banking and finance. He lives well but doesn't flaunt it, at least relative to some other billionaires.

Soros has given money to fight tuberculosis in Russian prisons. He supported get-out-the-vote movements in the United States. He funded media watchdog groups, Zimbabwean dissidents, refugee relief organizations. He created Open Society Foundations to promote democracy, freedom of expression and respect for individual rights. He has written fifteen books on investing, capitalism, globalization and philanthropy. His money and his expertise have allowed him a soapbox, and his tendency to support progressive causes such as justice, education, public health and independent media have long made him a target.

But it was following the US invasion of Iraq in 2002, when he became a vocal critic of US President George W. Bush and his administration, that he became a favourite of US Democrats and a perceived enemy of Republicans. And then the right-wing conspiracy theorists pounced. They've been relentless ever since. He's been the target of anti-Semitism, labelled a globalist, a left-wing radical, and "his name is invoked as an all-purpose symbol of liberalism run amok," according to the *New York Times*. In 2018, someone delivered an explosive device to his home in New York. Soros is hated by the right the same way the industrialist Charles Koch is hated by the left: mostly for his political leanings, real or imagined.

While politics always generates a heightened animosity, rich people don't need to be involved in politics or political commentary to be hated. Martha Stewart, once famous for her catchphrase "It's a good thing," knows that all too well. Declared "the definitive woman of our time" by *New York* magazine in 1995, the author, magazine editor and television personality turned her name into a brand for household greatness by the end of the twentieth century. She seemed to be everywhere at once, telling people how to bake, decorate, even plant trees. Her company, Martha Stewart Living, went public in 1999, elevating her instantly to billionaire status. To the general public, she came across as a smart, thoughtful, stylish, kindly, unflappable expert, perfect in every way.

But perhaps too perfect.

In 2003, Stewart was indicted for securities fraud related to insider trading, and found herself in the middle of a highly publicized trial. The government alleged she used insider information to sell her shares of ImClone, a biopharmaceutical company, to spare herself a loss of $45,000 when the stock dropped in price. She went to prison for five months as the public—and the media—piled on. At the time of her conviction, her lawyer said Stewart "has been scorned, ridiculed, and become the butt of all forms of derogatory publicity."

Supporters claimed she was singled out for her celebrity. For detractors, however, it was just deserts for a holier-than-thou rich and famous person they'd all had just about enough of. Both have merit. We can't know exactly how many other lesser-known beings have gotten away with insider trading, and indeed how many rich people have illegally profited through greater financial misdeeds, but it's a safe bet that Stewart's trespasses were relatively minor by comparison.

One might well wonder why Stewart, with her many millions, somehow felt it was wise to wade into a stock market quagmire that might save her a mere $45,000. But again, rich people aren't as smart as we think, and like the rest of us, they are tempted by easy money, no matter how much they already have (see Reason No. 5). On the other hand, like so many other celebrities, she used fame to propel her fortunes higher, so she was obliged to accept the barrage when it brought her down (see Reason No. 1). Humanity loves a downfall as much as a success story.

The world witnessed a different kind of downfall in the case of disgraced newspaper baron Conrad Black v. United States, but the media frenzy was even more intense. Born into wealth in Toronto, Black might have lived a life of quiet luxury, running his father's company, a successful conglomerate that owned a variety of interests, including a grocery store chain, a farm-machinery manufacturer and a brewery.

But Black wanted influence beyond the Canadian establishment of rich industry leaders; he wanted to be heard across the world. So he sold off the old companies, and by the end of the twentieth century had transformed himself into a high-flying newspaper mogul with media holdings across the globe, from Britain's *Telegraph* to the *Chicago Sun-Times* to the *Jerusalem Post*. He started the *National Post* in Canada and began pontificating widely on politics and free enterprise.

Though he would later say, preposterously, that "I never held myself as an especially wealthy man," he had a fortune estimated in the hundreds of millions—and a lifestyle to match. With his wife, the controversial and conservative journalist Barbara Amiel, he was unapologetically ostentatious (the couple once famously attended a costume ball at Kensington Palace dressed as Cardinal Richelieu and Marie Antoinette). He kept homes in Toronto, New York, Palm Beach and London, and happily showcased them for the media and a curious public.

Still, as it is with so many other rich people, all those homes and all that power wasn't enough. Black sought a British peerage, and to get it, he renounced his Canadian citizenship in 2001, adopting the title Lord Black of Crossharbour, which seemed to further annoy ordinary folk. Not long after that, his life began to unravel. Finally, his vast newspaper empire slipped away, he was charged with fraud and embezzlement, and he went to jail for obstruction of justice.

Black has insisted all along that he did nothing illegal, and most of the charges were later dropped, but by that time it hardly mattered. He was engulfed by a relentless tsunami of media coverage for years, endured a trial that lasted more than five months and spent tens of millions defending himself. His reputation, already under siege from various biographers, journalists, investors and jealous entrepreneurs, was in tatters, at least as far as the general public was concerned. There was more than a little *schadenfreude* involved, and as with Stewart, it was obvious that his fame, his pontificating and his perceived self-importance did him no favours as a voracious press and public gleefully picked apart every detail of his misery. A fellow columnist of Black's at Canada's *National Post* newspaper, the well-respected journalist Robert Fulford, described the situation succinctly as the legal saga began: "Can anyone remember one person bringing as much happiness to Canadians as Conrad Black has recently provided?"

There is a special place for media moguls in the hearts of haters. And the first in modern times may have been the contemptible William Randolph Hearst, inventor of so-called yellow journalism at the end of the nineteenth century. Like so many others whose money (and power) went to their heads, he had many enemies, few friends and lots of problems.

Famous for printing lurid tales about ne'er-do-wells, creating fake interviews and distorting events, his papers ran stories promoting anti-Asian racism, while allowing Nazis such as Hermann Göring and even Adolf Hitler to write unchallenged in his papers. Paranoid and power-hungry, Hearst tried with some success to influence politics and world affairs, and (again with some success) to prevent the distribution of one of the most admired films of all time, *Citizen Kane*, directed by and starring Orson Welles, because he thought it depicted him.

A control freak with others, but a monumental overshopper when he was alone, his collections filled warehouses. Hearst had ongoing money troubles, was once forced to sell almost everything to avoid bankruptcy, and for a time had to rent space in his own mansion in Los Angeles, the scene of many parties featuring Hollywood's A-listers. The downfall was music to the ears of many of his enemies, and the media, who covered it mercilessly. "He was shorn of financial control, bankrupted out of Hollywood, deprived of a castle and auctioneers were putting his treasures under the hammer," wrote a biographer. "Above all, he was being forced to do a thousand things he didn't want to do."

Robert Maxwell, who once owned Mirror Group Newspapers

in Britain, was an inspiration (among others) for the fictional arch-villain and evil media magnate Elliot Carver, who faced James Bond in the movie *Tomorrow Never Dies*. Once known as a left-leaning, high-flying, much-hated press baron, he mysteriously disappeared off the side of his yacht in 1991 as his company faced financial ruin under heavy debts and financial mismanagement. He may be just as famous today as the father of socialite Ghislaine Maxwell, an associate of the notorious sexual predator Jeffrey Epstein who is now in jail for sex trafficking, among other things.

Maxwell's successor as owner of the Mirror Group is an even bigger media fish, and probably even more reviled. Rupert Murdoch is the boss of News Corp, a worldwide publishing company that owns newspapers including the *Wall Street Journal*, Britain's the *Times* and the *Sun*, and Fox News, among many other properties. In 2011, he was obliged to tell Wall Street analysts that "there can be no doubt about our commitment to ethics and integrity"—the implication being, of course, that there was indeed great doubt.

That was in the wake of the infamous British phone-hacking scandal, wherein the public learned that journalists had routinely bought information from private investigators and helped hack into the mobile phones of private citizens. The phone-hacking scandal was a particular problem for Murdoch. It roiled the British political establishment, outraged readers, irked advertisers, inflamed the general public and revealed a rat's nest of misdeeds at the *News of the World*, a financially successful Murdoch property that closed as a result. In 2012, he was forced to resign as head of News Corp and cancel the company's proposed takeover of the British satellite broadcaster BSkyB. And he felt obliged to apologize. "I failed" and "I am very sorry for it," he said.

In all, more than two hundred people were targeted by the phone hackers, including actors like Sienna Miller, Jude Law, Angelina Jolie and Hugh Grant, and musicians like Eric Clapton and Mick Jagger.

Hackers also went after phones associated with politicians, sports icons and various royals. For years, Murdoch had been quietly paying off many of them and insisting on their silence, while claiming stories about the scandal were overblown. The scandal entangled politicians and police investigators, and it revealed an illegal, unethical and cozy relationship between the press, the police and politicians. As well, it demonstrated the need for better media safeguards. But the incident that broke the scandal wide open, enraged the public, brought down the newspaper, cost the company millions and eventually forced Murdoch's apology did not involve a rich or famous person. It had in fact occurred a decade earlier, when hackers had found their way into the voice-mail inbox of Milly Dowler, a thirteen-year-old who had disappeared in 2002, and whose body was discovered five months later.

When the *Guardian*, the newspaper that had long been investigating the hacking scandal, wrote about that in 2011, the public outrage grew exponentially. Still trying to contain the crisis after shutting down the *News of the World* shortly thereafter, Murdoch took out ads in national newspapers headlined "We are sorry." The apology continued, "We are sorry for the serious wrongdoing that occurred. We are deeply sorry for the hurt suffered by the individuals affected." It was signed by Murdoch himself.

Today, little has changed, much to the dismay of Nick Davies, the *Guardian* reporter who covered the scandal back then. He believes legislators lost an opportunity to rein in Murdoch's political power. "But you know, power doesn't relax its grip easily," he said in a 2021 *Guardian* piece on the scandal's anniversary. "And slowly and insidiously Murdoch got his bony fingers back around the throat of British public life and has kept them there." Murdoch has often insisted the activities of the *News of the World* were the result of rogue editors and do not reflect the way his companies do business. But a year after his famous apologies, he was secretly taped railing against the investigation, saying "the cops are incompetent" and "it's the biggest inquiry ever, over next to nothing."

Media moguls easily attract animosity because their influence is more public. Sometimes, though, the nefarious doings of the rich take some time to come to light. The secretive Sackler family, which *Forbes* says is one of the richest in the United States, was long known for philanthropic projects far and wide. The name was pasted on museums around the world, including the Tate in London, the Met in New York and the Louvre in Paris; and on health and educational facilities at places like MIT, Columbia and Stanford, among many others. But when it came to discussing the source of all that money, they weren't terribly keen.

It originated with the purchase of a small drug maker in the 1950s by three Sackler brothers, Arthur, Mortimer and Raymond, all of whom were entrepreneurial physicians. The company prospered, making the brothers and their families rich. Arthur died in 1987, and his family cashed out. Shortly thereafter, the company became known as Purdue Pharma, and in 1995, it developed OxyContin, destroyer of lives, families and entire communities across the United States and Canada—and a spigot that poured billions into the coffers of the two surviving brothers and their families.

Doctors had always been careful around opioids, well aware of their addictive nature, and prescribed them only for severe cancer cases and those facing death. But Purdue, already an expert at pushing drugs, aggressively marketed its powerful new pain-killer. The company downplayed the risks and talked up the benefits, deceiving physicians into believing OxyContin was useful for a wide variety of ailments and dishonestly insisting that concerns about dependency were exaggerated.

Soon, patients were addicted to OxyContin, many started abusing it, and others trafficked it on the black market. The result was billions in sales, millions of addicts, hundreds of thousands of deaths and a public-health crisis that stretched across borders, bringing tragedy and misery to countless communities unable to afford the fallout. In a scenario strangely reminiscent of tobacco companies more than a generation earlier, Purdue initially defended the product and its marketing.

Since then, as the opioid crisis continues to rage across the continent, things have gone poorly for Purdue, and for the family. The company pleaded guilty to felony charges in 2007 for misleading doctors, paying a $600-million fine that observers quickly recognized as a mere slap on the wrist. Indeed, it was just the beginning. More than a decade later, the company and the family contemplated payouts ten times that figure. They have expressed regret but have not apologized for their role in the opioid crisis, while being accused of manipulating the bankruptcy system, misappropriating funds and getting special treatment because they are billionaires.

In a testy exchange at a hearing in 2020 before the US House of Representatives Committee on Oversight and Reform, David Sackler, a Purdue board member, was accused by Carolyn Maloney, chair of the committee, of withdrawing more than $10 billion from Purdue as lawsuits piled up across the country, and hiding money offshore, before Purdue filed for bankruptcy protection. "I think it's fair that your family has tried to fraudulently shield money for your own personal benefit," said Maloney. "I think it's appalling. Those profits, in my opinion, should be clawed back. You and your family should compensate the American public for the harm that you've caused, and you should be held fully accountable for your actions."

The Sacklers eventually proposed a payment of as much as $6 billion in exchange for immunity from further lawsuits, but nothing has yet been settled, except, perhaps, the family's future as benevolent philanthropists. Their reputation is now in ruins, they are at war with each other and their money is considered dirty.

Many charities will not accept it today. The Louvre in Paris and the National Gallery in London, among others, have removed signs displaying the Sackler name, partly because of demonstrations and activism by New York photographer Nan Goldin, who became aware of the family after being prescribed OxyContin and recovering from an addiction to it. "I don't know how they live with themselves," Goldin said in 2018.

The rich and powerful often can't see the realities the rest of the world considers obvious. Perhaps that's because they think they have more information than ordinary people, or because they think they know best, or because they choose to ignore the obvious. John D. Rockefeller could be accused of all of that. The famously ruthless oil tycoon thought of himself as a practical business operator, a friendly competitor, a kindly employer and a thoughtful philanthropist.

Unlike most rich people, including his contemporary Andrew Carnegie, Rockefeller began giving away money when he was still a teenager, and in his twenties he was donating more than 10 per cent of his income to charity. As a young man, he was known to be reserved, religious and thoughtful. He considered a career in music.

As he got older, he became ruthless, relentless, cold-blooded and unrepentant on his way to creating Standard Oil, a monopoly later deemed illegal and broken up under court order, making Rockefeller even richer, if not as powerful. Rockefeller had crushed competitors, concentrated power and ruined livelihoods in building his company in the late 1800s.

By the turn of the century, public sentiment had turned against him, as it had for so many other rich people before—and since. Especially damning was a 1904 book by the muckraking journalist Ida M. Tarbell, *The History of the Standard Oil Company*, which outlined in cold, dispassionate detail the company's take-no-prisoners approach. Rockefeller was livid about Tarbell's reporting, calling her "that poisonous woman." But he was also upset about his various critics and about the breakup of his company, because he simply couldn't see himself as others did: greedy, aloof, imperious, even diabolical.

He set out to change that, launching a public-relations campaign and writing a memoir, neither of which did much to improve perceptions. But where those failed, philanthropy may have succeeded, and he had lots of time to work at it. Rockefeller lived to be ninety-seven and was probably never as happy in those many decades of retirement as he was when fully engaged in business. "It is wrong to assume that men of immense wealth are always happy" is a quote often attributed to him.

Eventually, his reputation as a ruthless oil baron faded as his philanthropy flourished. He gave $500 million to various universities, to public health organizations, medical research and training, education and the arts. Is he better known today as a kindly philanthropist or an evil entrepreneur? He would likely be disappointed to learn that today most people recall him as neither—he's remembered simply for being rich.

Nothing Is Inevitable

"Why wouldn't we want to live longer if you're living really great?"
—James Strole, a self-described "anti-death activist"

Reason No. 9 is that rich people grow old and die, just like the rest of us.

Most of us, rich or poor, want to live forever—to avoid death is instinctive. And nobody has ever enjoyed getting old. The quest for the mythical fountain of youth, made famous by Spanish explorer Ponce de León in the fifteenth century, goes back at least 2,500 years, appearing in the writings of Herodotus in ancient Greece, and likely before that. Rich people, as usual, have led the search. And why not? Their fabulous lives are coming to an end. They'll do anything to extend an existence marked by affluence and abundance.

In ancient Egypt, the poor may have been buried in pits or left to the scavengers in the desert, but the wealthy had their bodies carefully mummified and their elaborate tombs packed with luxury items, so if the gods allowed them to ascend into the afterlife, they'd have everything they needed. Thousands of years later, Europeans for centuries before the Second World War were prescribed powders and potions made from those decaying mummies. Winston Churchill and Noël Coward were said to be among those who made discreet trips to Switzerland to be injected with cells from unborn lambs to ward off aging.

Today, nothing much has changed. But the merely wealthy (as opposed to the superrich) with limited retirement funds are haunted by the misery that may await us in old age: overcrowded hospitals, dreary seniors' homes, or life in some remote community where the rent is cheap but the weather questionable and the services scarce. We can't afford a rotating staff of personal caregivers, an accessible one-floor house with ramps and railings, or even those machines that haul us up and down the stairs in our so-called golden years, let alone the conveniences that await multimillionaires. The most practical among us simply accept the reality that death is coming and probably won't be pretty. We reluctantly come to grips with the inevitable, and we console ourselves that we've been lucky enough to survive six or eight decades already.

The rich think differently. Just as they don't accept the necessity of taxes, they don't believe in the inevitability of old age or even death. It is a fact that rich people live longer than poor people. In the United States, the richest 1 per cent live almost fifteen years longer than the poorest 1 per cent. In Canada, those with high incomes can expect to live eight years longer than those with low incomes. It's not surprising. Rich people get better health care. They eat better food. They exercise more, and they seem to have more fun doing it. They have the time and the means to take care of themselves, mentally and physically.

The superrich do all that and then some. They have personal chefs or dine out at expensive restaurants that make spinach and tofu taste good so they aren't tempted by French fries and pizza. They have personal trainers who drag them into high-tech gyms daily. They can afford Peloton exercise machines in the basement, lap pools in the backyard and private tennis courts behind the hedgerow. They need not wait for hours with poor people in chaotic emergency rooms or overcrowded clinics; they have personal health-care professionals at their beck and call: doctors, dentists, surgeons, therapists, psychiatrists, pharmacists, herbologists, naturopaths, masseuses, dieticians, acupuncturists and other helpers (see Reason No. 2), all of whom visit them regularly in the privacy of their gracious homes to relieve their aches and pains, buttress their physiology or just make sure everything is shipshape.

Even that is not enough. Humans want not just to feel well but to look that way. We don't want to be reminded of our old age when we look in the mirror, at selfies or on Instagram posts. But rich people have more opportunities—and more time—to consider their appearance, more discretionary income to fix it, and perhaps more peer pressure to act. Their solution is often cosmetic surgery: a bit of Botox maybe, a nose job perhaps, a tummy tuck here or a butt lift there. The result is that despite their best efforts, many rich people do not age gracefully, and certainly not naturally. Resilient actor and writer Jamie Lee Curtis, whose plastic surgery treatments got her addicted to Vicodin, does not have much good to say about it: "The current trend of fillers and procedures, and this obsession with filtering, and the things we do to adjust our appearance on Zoom are wiping out generations of beauty. Once you mess with your face you can't get it back."

Messing with your face becomes necessary for some people who mess too much with their bodies. The demand for face fillers is growing, not only because rich people are getting old, but because of the current vogue for thinness and the popularity of diabetes drugs such as Ozempic and Mounjaro, which are being used to treat obesity. Despite costs that can run to $1,000 a month, these drugs are in growing demand because they work quickly and with less effort than normal dieting. In addition to other side effects, however, losing weight can make the face look old and gaunt, a symptom increasingly known among users and some doctors as

"Ozempic face." Paul Jarrod Frank, a New York dermatologist, told the *New York Times* "it's the drug of choice these days for the one per cent."

Plastic surgery is nothing new; it has been practised in one form or another for millennia. Broken noses were being repaired more than three thousand years ago in Egypt. "Reconstructive art" was being done in India two thousand years ago. Reconstructive surgery occurred in isolated cases in Italy in the sixteenth century. But things picked up speed during the First World War, when horribly maimed soldiers required various bodily reconstructions, and doctors did what they could to put them back together. It has been growing exponentially since the 1960s, when the monied set realized a better body could lead to a better life.

Today, cosmetic surgery worldwide is worth more than $40 billion a year by some estimates—and growing. From Brazil to South Korea, vain rich people and ambitious (or desperate) poorer people are expected by the end of the decade to spend more than $70 billion on artificially augmenting their bodies. We're obsessed with almost every part of our exteriors, it seems, and it just so happens there's a solution to almost every problem we perceive, and a steep price to go with it. "We as a society somehow leapfrogged from 'Wow, that plastic surgery is so extreme' to 'when are you getting your plastic surgery,'" said Justine Bateman, a filmmaker and actor who gained fame in the 1980s as a cheerful teen on the sitcom *Family Ties* and the author of *Face: One Square Foot of Skin*.

Decades ago, plastic surgery tended to happen discreetly and was rarely discussed; now it is often a badge of honour for those wealthy enough to afford it, bragged about on social media and talked about frankly in celebrity interviews. Kaley Cuoco, who played a perky non-egghead on television's *The Big Bang Theory*, admits to having her nose done, and happily adds that enhancing her breasts was the "best thing I ever did."

Uber-celebrity Kim Kardashian's Botox treatment was featured on her reality TV show, sending thousands, perhaps millions, of viewers for similar treatment. Cynthia Bailey and Sonja Morgan, stars of Bravo's *Real Housewives* franchise, underwent vaginal rejuvenation for a television audience. "I'm very happy," said Kelly Dodd, star of *The Real Housewives of Orange County*, who had the procedure done on an episode in 2017. She added that her "husband likes it—it's good."

In a world obsessed by such details, and such fame, it's not uncommon for ordinary rich patients to arrive for an appointment with the plastic surgeon carrying a photograph of their favourite movie star or fashion model. And while speculation abounds about the extent to which plastic surgery has consumed Hollywood, there is considerable evidence that not all of it has gone particularly well. Shape-shifting personalities such as socialite Jocelyn Wildenstein, pioneering musician Michael Jackson, fashionista Donatella Versace and country crooner Kenny Rogers are often singled out for sympathy, curiosity or ridicule. The blunt-talking TV personality Simon Cowell said he stopped using face fillers after realizing he looked "like something out of a horror film."

Supermodel Linda Evangelista, famous for the quote "We don't wake up for less than $10,000 a day," revealed on Instagram in 2021 that a process called CoolSculpting left her "permanently deformed" and "brutally disfigured." Painful corrective surgeries were unsuccessful, she wrote, and she developed paradoxical adipose hyperplasia as a result, which "has not only destroyed my livelihood, it has sent me into a cycle of deep depression, profound sadness, and the lowest depths of self-loathing."

Such outcomes are bad enough if you are terrifically rich, but the merely moderately rich face a quandary. They had enough money to get the original procedure, but they lack the funds for remedial work. Consequently, and in typically North American fashion, many find themselves in front of a television audience on such grisly yet popular cable shows as *Botched*, which has been running for eight seasons.

For most of my life, I have been blessed with a body that functions reasonably well. Modern medicine and skilled surgeons have fixed—twice—a heart defect I was born with, and extended my life by five decades and counting. I never smoked tobacco, I eat better than most and I get a moderate amount of exercise. I do not have a movie-star face (or body), but neither am I a movie star, so I haven't felt the need to fuss over myself. I am not much of an athlete, was never much for exercise machines or weight training. I hate doing push-ups, sit-ups, knee-bends and the like, despite their obvious benefits. But I walk a lot, as much for mental health as physical. Most of the hair on my head disappeared when I was in my twenties, which I considered then as now a bit of a curse, but relatively speaking, it's hardly a burden.

Like most balding men, I was once intrigued by hair transplants, but never seriously considered it, nor did I ever feel I had the money or the courage for such a procedure. And I am tall by most standards, an advantage I have not always been conscious of, but an attribute I am reminded of increasingly in an age when "height surgery," in which one's legs are broken and steel pins inserted at great expense, and perhaps great pain, is gaining popularity. More than anything, however, I am blessed with reasonable mental health, the ability to be happy with what I have been given and live in the moment, and the good sense to know that wanting more will not solve my issues and that a simple life can be the richest of all.

It's not so easy for the superrich, and especially for the famous. They are under more scrutiny than the rest of us. Business leaders feel the need to present a facade of invincibility. Actors are constantly sized up by directors and audiences. Politicians are surveyed endlessly by the media and the electorate. And all of them face interminable comments, good and bad, on social media. Who knows what influence their social circles have on them, but it's likely they all receive more than your average amount of peer pressure to be perfect.

On many occasions as a boy, while trailing my father, a Canadian television personality, in public places, I would overhear passersby say under their breaths that "he looks better on TV." No kidding, I would think to myself: he's plastered in makeup, wearing a nice suit, smiling for all and sundry and basking in studio lighting meant to show his best side, rather than schlepping his ragtag family and their cumbersome baggage through the airport or crowding into a roadside diner for lunch. No wonder so many people feel they must transform into their new and improved selves when they go to the supermarket. In a social media world where everyone is carrying a camera and using it incessantly, we're all getting progressively more famous.

Pam Behan, an employee of the Kardashian and Jenner family before they became omnipresent media stars, says she felt the pressure for plastic improvement while living in their midst. Caitlyn Jenner, the Olympic gold medallist then known as Bruce, once told her she should consider rhinoplasty. "You should probably have a little taken off your nose," Behan quoted him as saying. "Huh?" wrote Behan in her memoir, *Malibu Nanny: Adventures of the Former Kardashian Nanny*. "I'm nineteen. It had never, ever occurred to me that I might need a nose job...I guess in the land of the beautiful and perfect people, there was always some 'work' that could be done."

It is in such milieus, therefore, that prescribed appearances can be key to a successful career and a happy life. In a moment of honesty uncharacteristic of many movie stars, the former sex symbol and legendary activist Jane Fonda said in 2018 that she wasn't proud of various cosmetic improvements she had visited upon herself: "On one level, I hate the fact that I've had the need to alter myself physically to feel that I'm okay. I wish I wasn't like that."

For some rich people, looking good into old age is not enough. They want to feel good and look good *forever* and, if they have enough money, they believe they just might be able to achieve it. Every year since 2016, so-called radical life extension enthusiasts join scientists, philanthropists, futurists, researchers, clinicians, bioengineers and various rich people from around the world at an event called RAADfest (or Revolution Against Aging and Death).

It's billed as the world's largest event focused on anti-aging and age-reversal science for a general audience. For several days, a thousand or more pilgrims crowd into an upscale hotel and convention centre to brainstorm about how to live longer while shopping at nearby kiosks for equipment and treatments to assist in their quest. A lead organizer is James Strole, executive director of the Coalition for Radical Life Extension, an author and a self-described "visionary anti-death activist." In explaining the popularity of the event, Strole once articulated what many rich people must feel: "Why wouldn't we want to live longer if you're living really great?"

Dave Asprey, a presenter at the event in recent years, is one of many high-profile evangelists for the cause. Asprey is rich, because, as he tells followers in one of many videos, "I worked at the company that held Google's first servers when Google was two servers and two guys." In due course, he "was able to spend myself to wellness" and commit himself to "getting younger." He expects to live to 180, and he sounds confident about it. But to accomplish this, the self-help author, inspirational podcaster and lifestyle guru uses multifarious methods, from fasting and a regimen of health supplements to drinking Bulletproof coffee, a high-fat concoction he invented that helped make him famous (and richer).

Asprey, a self-described "biohacker," has injected himself with his own stem cells, which were removed from bone marrow taken from his hips, a procedure he once said he planned to repeat every six months. In his house on Vancouver Island, he has a cryotherapy chamber, an atmospheric cell trainer, an infrared bed and various other nifty-looking, high-tech machines he claims will roll back the years. And he rents this stuff out by the hour to others who want to live forever. Needless to say, it's not cheap.

Neither is buying blood, a process sometimes disparagingly labelled "modern vampirism." That unpleasant description did not stop rich older people from buying the stuff from (presumably poor) younger people for $8,000 a litre in 2018. It enjoyed a brief moment of media attention before the US Food and Drug Administration declared that young blood has "no proven clinical benefit." Today, old blood remains a rich person's problem.

Other hopeful multimillionaires, while unconvinced of their ability to live much past eighty or ninety, are hoping that the emerging field of brain preservation might offer a chance for some kind of renewed life in the future. Referencing a process called aldehyde-stabilized cryopreservation, some claimed in 2018 that information in the mind could somehow be saved before—presumably *just* before—death and then, perhaps sometime in the future, uploaded into a computer. It is as expensive as it is complex.

Despite the skepticism from various corners, the promise of immortality or an abnormally long life continues to mesmerize rich people. At least not at a mere ninety or one hundred years of age. After all, they figure, if a giant tortoise or a bowhead whale can live two hundred years, why not humans?

For them, death is not a fact of life, and it is not inevitable; it is a problem. And like so many problems of the rich, the solution is to throw money at it. In his book *Homo Deus*, Yuval Noah Harari observes that humanity has been trained to observe various ailments as "technical problems" for which there can be a solution.

Doctors, he notes cleverly, are likely to tell patients they have the flu or cancer or various other ailments. "But the doctor will never say 'you have death.'"

When the rich set their sights on something, they are generally pretty good at finding, following or financing smart people to help tackle their problems, whether it be death, taxes or something else. Silicon Valley has been a hotbed for start-ups and biotech firms with dreams of stopping the inexorable march of the Grim Reaper, and those attracting the attention of billionaires include controversial gerontologist Aubrey de Grey and Ray Kurzweil, an eminent computer scientist, among other impressive things. Both are among a growing group of smart scientists, hopeful futurists and rich entrepreneurs who believe death, at least from natural causes, is not inevitable. Kurzweil joined Google a decade ago as director of engineering before Google founders Sergey Brin and Larry Page helped launch Calico, which aims to "better understand the biology that controls aging and lifespan" and "enable people to live longer and healthier lives."

Amazon's Jeff Bezos, among others, has invested in Unity Biotechnology, which wants to "slow, halt or reverse diseases of aging." Its research with so-called senescent cells has had some promising results—with mice. For billionaire Oracle founder Larry Ellison, who has donated hundreds of millions to aging research, dying is a challenge that must be overcome: "Death has never made any sense to me."

In his exhaustive investigation of humanity's obsession with eternal life, *The Book of Immortality: The Science, Belief, and Magic Behind Living Forever,* Adam Leith Gollner is skeptical of humanity's ability to cheat death indefinitely. Because we so desperately want to live forever, we look for evidence that we can, he argues. We should not overestimate the abilities of science to answer the biggest questions of our existence, he says, noting that "scientific immortalism isn't scientific; it's belief clothed in scientific garb. Eternal life, whether in this world or the next, is always a story about our inability to comprehend death."

Perhaps this is why rich people believe they can live forever. They've had such success in life, or believe they have, that anything appears possible. There is perhaps no billionaire more associated with such endeavours than Peter Thiel, the co-founder of PayPal and Palantir Technologies, among other ventures. His $500,000 investment in Facebook in 2004 netted him more than $1 billion when he sold his shares in 2012. His money funds a variety of anti-aging organizations, including the Methuselah Foundation, a non-profit that hopes to make "90 the new 50 by 2030."

Never one to put all his eggs in one basket, Thiel, like more than one thousand other rich people, has also registered with the Alcor Life Extension Foundation. Since the 1970s, Alcor has been freezing dead people (and sometimes just their heads) for fees in the hundreds of thousands, plus annual dues, so when modern medical science finally does construct a fail-safe fountain of youth, the dearly departed can somehow be rejuvenated, reanimated, have their brains uploaded to a computer or maybe even jolted to life like some kind of Frankenstein monster. Thiel, now in his fifties, hopes to live to 120. "Death," he said once, "will eventually be reduced from a mystery to a solvable problem."

Many critics shake their heads at these schemes. A lot of scientists are skeptical. And even some rich people are appalled: as Bill Gates told a Reddit audience in 2015, "It seems pretty egocentric, while we still have malaria and TB, for rich people to fund things so they can live longer." In his book *Heavens on Earth: The Scientific Search for the Afterlife, Immortality, and Utopia*, Michael Shermer concludes that "facing death—and life—with courage, awareness and honesty can bring out the best in us and focus our minds on what matters most: gratitude and love."

But more and more rich people are becoming convinced some of these solutions are at hand. And to be fair, despite the usual assortment of hare-brained theories and snake-oil promises, it is reasonable to assume that some of it might just work. After all, even poor people live longer today than a century ago. Since 1900, the global average life expectancy has more than doubled. So it's a fair bet we will all be living longer—and better—in the future, and particularly so if we are rich. Good news for many individuals, though not necessarily ideal for a planet with an exploding human population. It's impossible to predict future growth or what population the planet can manage, but human crowding amid scarce resources rarely ends well.

Still, just because modern medicine, life-science start-ups or various life-extending technologies may allow some of us to live healthily to 150 or 200, it doesn't mean we'll be living happily. We may have reduced the chances of probable death from natural causes, but we still worry about possible death from unnatural ones—and true to form, the billionaires are plotting a solution (at least for themselves) to this problem too.

Rich people like to anticipate things (indeed, that's why many of them are rich), so they can avoid unpleasantness or make the best of it. They know that while money is often helpful when you are in a tight spot, all that cash is for naught when the boat is sinking, or the airplane is falling out of the sky, or the bombs are dropping. That's why they buy the best boats and planes, the best radar equipment and the most seasoned captains.

It's why they feel obliged to whisper in the ears of politicians, lobby governments or help finance certain election campaigns. It's also why they build panic rooms in their urban mansions and nuclear fallout shelters at their country estates to spare them from everyday local nastiness or a possible worldwide apocalypse. You just never know. After Russia invaded Ukraine, the demand for luxury fallout bunkers, already brisk, went through the roof. Brian Camden, the owner of Hardened Structures in Virginia, where business in luxury shelters is booming, is just one of many entrepreneurs who has enjoyed increased attention from the media in recent years: "Asteroids, the antichrist, nuclear fallout, Armageddon," he told one reporter. "Our team is not here to judge, but rather to find out the client's priorities and make them our priorities."

Guy Laliberté, the former busker who started Cirque de Soleil, can relate. In 2007, the professional poker-playing billionaire bought Nukutepipi, an atoll in French Polynesia, and told a reporter in 2014 exactly why: "Because of all that's happening in the world, I said to myself, that could be the place where, in case of an epidemic or a total war, I could bring people I like and my family so that we'd be protected."

Unfortunately for Laliberté, the paradise became a problem for him in 2019, when he was arrested for cannabis cultivation on the island. Possession of marijuana is illegal in French Polynesia. He apparently grows it there for personal use and issued a statement saying he was surprised by the "disproportionate importance given to this matter" (see Reason No. 1).

Peter Thiel also seems to be hedging his bets. In 2011, the German-American entrepreneur quietly became a citizen of New Zealand. Normally, such a privilege is granted after a stringent application process, and hopefuls must live in the country for at least 1,350 days over five years. But that doesn't necessarily apply to rich people. Thiel somehow acquired his citizenship after less than two weeks in the country, on the basis of his philanthropy and entrepreneurship, and his ability to promote the country to the world. At the time, he had no plans to settle in New Zealand, but it's not easy for foreigners to own land there.

By 2016, it was revealed that Thiel had set his sights on New Zealand not just because of its natural beauty or remote location, but also because it could provide him with an ideal perch from which to wait out whatever political, environmental or medical apocalypse he foresees in his worst nightmares. In fact, New Zealand has been oddly identified by others as an emergency refuge for rich people who might be worried the world is not unfolding as they think it should. Today, Thiel owns a remote former sheep station on 477 acres on New Zealand's sparsely populated South Island. But he has been unable to convince the local council to allow him to build a vast complex of buildings on the pristine site. In 2022, his application to develop the property, complete with low-slung dwellings discreetly built into hillsides and partially hidden from view (and perhaps protected by the landscape itself), was denied because too many locals complained it would spoil the landscape.

It's not just that humans are afraid of death or want to live forever. That's instinct. Maybe it's because we've been trained to be fearful by centuries of proselytizing sermons, gruesome fairy tales, terrifying horror movies and various unpleasant depictions of our departure from this world. We've been told endlessly that a better life awaits us.

Even if that's not the case, some existences—and some deaths —can provide individuals with a kind of immortality. It may be why so many of us chase fame. Even if the teenaged King Tut, for example, did not settle comfortably into eternal existence with all his stuff, he certainly lives on in our minds three thousand years later, easily more famous today than he ever was when he ruled Egypt.

Perhaps that's all we really want—to be remembered? The question is how to accomplish it.

In 1961, Anthony Burgess, while writing the disturbing and dystopian novel *A Clockwork Orange*, scrawled a note to himself, or perhaps to his editor, in the margin of his original manuscript: "Will this name be known when book appears?" The name was

Elvis Presley. The book was published less than a year later. The passage, on page eight of the original manuscript, mentioned other names, but ironically Presley's was the one that concerned Burgess: "We put our maskies on—new jobs these were, real horrorshow, wonderfully done really; they were like faces of historical personalities (they gave you the name when you bought) and I had Disraeli, Peter had Elvis Presley, Georgie had Henry VIII and poor old Dim had a poet Veck called Peebee Shelley."

Today, six decades later, Presley is considered one of the most significant cultural figures of the twentieth century. The bestselling solo music artist of all time, widely known around the world as the "King of Rock 'n' Roll," he still inspires legions of impersonators across the planet. When his daughter, Lisa Marie, a singer-songwriter mostly known for being Elvis's daughter, died in 2023 at fifty-four, the news made headlines for a week and warranted no fewer than six different stories in the *New York Times*. Graceland, Elvis's folksy mansion in Memphis, Tennessee, is a US National Historic Landmark. Hundreds of thousands of visitors tour the place each year, making it the second-most-visited home in the United States, second only to the White House.

Why do some people get fifteen minutes of fame and others achieve immortality? Why do more people today know Elvis than Benjamin Disraeli, the Conservative British prime minister, or Percy Bysshe Shelley, the ill-fated romantic poet, or even the murderous adulterer King Henry VIII?

My father hosted a television program called *The Pierre Berton Show* between 1962 and 1973. The program's modern claim to fame may be that it hosted the only known televised interview with Bruce Lee in 1971, a portion of which is frequently viewed on the internet. Among the others he featured over the years were such reliable icons as Malcolm X and Lenny Bruce, as well as those whose fame burned brightly for a much shorter period: Robert Culp, a busy actor who worked regularly in television for over three decades, and Susan Strasberg, daughter of the famous theatre director and drama coach Lee Strasberg. In 1955, Strasberg appeared on the covers of *Life* and *Newsweek*. In the 1960s and '70s, she appeared in endless movies and television shows, but by 1980, she had simply faded away, much to her chagrin. "I had played Juliet, Cleopatra and Anne Frank," she wrote in her memoir, "and there I was, sitting in Hollywood just waiting for somebody to want me."

Others who made appearances on *The Pierre Berton Show* include memorable actors such as Cicely Tyson and James Earl Jones, the prancing and persistent rocker Mick Jagger, and less enduring singer-actors Fabian and Lulu. He interviewed both Paula Prentiss and Richard Benjamin, once big stars who have been married to each other since 1961. Both are active in Hollywood to this day, but it's a good guess nobody recognizes them when they go out for dinner, and half the population probably doesn't know their names. In 1968, he interviewed Barbara Feldon, once a household name for her role as Agent 99 on the hit TV show *Get Smart*. In 2016, well into her eighties, Feldon reflected on the modern hysteria around fame: "What is the value of celebrity? It's an illusion. You can't eat it. You can't live it."

In 1999, *Time* magazine listed the "most important people" of the twentieth century. The list was compiled by a group of prominent A-listers—academics, politicians and journalists—but it is a bit of a dog's breakfast, undoubtedly influenced by the magazine's need to be commercial and inclusive, and a reflection, probably, of a lot of conflicting perspectives.

Yes, Rosa Parks is on the list, and Mother Teresa. And Albert Einstein was chosen the person of the century, but there are lots of celebrities on it too, and some have already faded from our collective consciousness. It's hard to imagine many of them making any list compiled at the end of the twenty-first century. Jane Russell and Marilyn Monroe were famously immortalized on the Hollywood Walk of Fame on the same day in 1953. Why does Monroe still occupy such a big part of our collective consciousness when Russell does not?

Not surprisingly, a lot of rich people, too, are featured. Bill Gates is there, but Steve Jobs is not. Jobs will be remembered in future for revolutionizing personal computers, because most of us can easily grasp (and visualize) that accomplishment. Despite all his achievements, Gates in future will be famous only for his money (and perhaps his philanthropy), because then (as probably now) people will not understand exactly how he earned it.

Most people know Vanderbilt and Astor and Carnegie and Rockefeller, if they know them at all, only for their money. They have no idea what they did to make it, though they might suspect that some of their methods were dubious, and some of their heirs were less than industrious. It's probably not the legacy they wanted to leave. How will others be remembered—for their art or their accomplishments or their sins? Or will they be remembered at all?

Will Che Guevara endure in the public consciousness longer than Fidel Castro, and if so, will that occur simply because of an iconic and copyright-free photograph on a poster and a T-shirt? Do most people even know what he did in life?

Who will be famous in future? Death remains a certainty for all of us, but many still grasp at immortality in various forms.

Isolation and Boredom

"Self-gratification does not last long enough and it does not turn into happiness."
—John Hervey, who inherited a fortune and died broke

Reason No. 10 is that money can't buy everything.

That's not to say money can't buy *almost* everything, because we all know it can. If you are rich, you can buy citizenship in some countries, or even a noble title. You can pay a surrogate mother to carry your baby. You can buy a kidney and even a liver or a cornea, even though it's illegal in most countries. You can pay to kill endangered species and convince yourself you're doing it for conservation. You can buy carbon credits that allow you to pollute, if you're not already polluting with impunity.

As for extravagance, the fabulously rich demonstrate they can push the envelope of consumerism. They can spend $50,000 or more on a single bottle of champagne, $80,000 a night for a hotel room, or $1 million to throw a party. They buy ever-bigger yachts, outrageously opulent dwellings, fleets of luxury cars and entire tropical islands, expenditures that are surely obscene in a world with escalating economic disparity. As Oscar Wilde said, "Nothing succeeds like excess."

Inevitably, though, that kind of opulent living somehow becomes dull. They must seek out new, better, more outrageous experiences, most of which are available only to the very rich: a trip to the upper atmosphere or beyond on an alleged spacecraft, perhaps. A dangerous ascent into thin air atop the world's tallest mountain. Or a submarine adventure to troll the depths of the ocean.

Action star Tom Cruise is an aerobatic pilot in what little spare time he seems to have. He owns a P-51 Mustang, a vintage Second World War fighter-bomber, among other aircraft. Fun-loving Virgin founder Richard Branson likes setting world records in hot-air balloons and on kiteboards. "McDreamy" actor Patrick Dempsey is one of many Hollywood stars who took up car racing in his spare time.

From time to time, these exotic hobbies go tragically wrong, and no amount of money can help. Iconic actor and wannabe racing-car driver James Dean famously died in a speeding Porsche in 1955. Stefano Casiraghi, a wealthy Italian financier and the husband of Princess Caroline of Monaco, died when his speedboat flipped during a race on the French Riviera in 1990.

Fresh-faced singer-songwriter John Denver liked to pilot aircraft, and he owned a collection of them. He died flying one in 1997, despite an FAA order prohibiting him from operating any aircraft due to several arrests for impaired driving.

Michael Rockefeller, a wealthy grandson of the famous financier John D. Rockefeller and a treasure hunter of Indigenous art, disappeared at age twenty-three in the jungles of what is now Papua New Guinea in 1961, probably killed by Indigenous people there, and possibly eaten by them. "It's the desire to do something adventurous," he said once, explaining his passion, but perhaps transmitting the real reason: boredom, a recurring issue for rich people.

Money can buy people an adventure, but it can't rescue them from an untimely death (see Reason No. 9) and can often facilitate it. Rich people and their poor helpers continue to die by the hundreds trying to reach the top of Mount Everest, K2 and other places in thin air, for reasons clear only to rich mountain climbers. Sandy Pittman, a New York socialite who had carefully nurtured a media profile, almost became one of them. She spent hundreds of thousands of dollars and years of her life climbing the world's tallest peaks, but escaped death in a highly publicized disaster on Everest in 1996 that killed eight fellow climbers. Instead of being able to celebrate her accomplishment and tell her own story, as she planned, it was told for her, and not at all to her liking: "I got pigeonholed as a rich New Yorker, and those three words, 'rich New Yorker' just painted such an easy picture of a villain right there."

But despite the risks, such activities allow rich people to meet other rich people, and they provide them with tales of far-flung adventures and derring-do to bring up at dinner parties or on social media.

It's certainly more exciting than the diversions of the moderately rich, like hiking in Peru, going on safari in Namibia or taking the bullet train in Japan. Even that is probably going to play better at the next social gathering than recounting a game of golf at the club, vacationing in the Poconos or going on a Caribbean cruise with thousands of other everyday rich and comfortable tourists, all of whom engage in such diversions with tedious regularity.

Broadcasting the highlights of our fabulous lives, whether we're rich or poor, is a hallmark of the twenty-first century and social media, the modern equivalent of the interminable 1960s slide show. But when so many are already awash in so much money, and unrelenting personal updates are coming at us with blinding speed from various social media platforms, it's difficult to be heard amid the din. Indulging in rarefied activities makes this easier, but, as always, it's often not enough. Eventually, many of the superrich become unhappy and frustrated, and they begin looking for something more. Unsatisfied with life, they descend into depression.

In fact, instances of substance abuse, depression and anxiety among the wealthy exceed national averages. How is this possible? Until recently, nobody believed it, save the rich themselves, and typically, they are reluctant to discuss such matters, and not only because they know they won't get much sympathy from those less financially fortunate. A half century ago, there was very little, if any, research on mental challenges facing the wealthy. After all, there have always been more poor people than rich people, and it is only recently that the population of really rich people has started to explode. Since then, studying and documenting rich people's mental-health problems has become something of a cottage industry.

There are now libraries full of scholarly articles on the topic of rich people's problems. One of the more famous is "The Joys and Dilemmas of Wealth." Produced by Boston College's Center on Wealth and Philanthropy, which began delving into the issue in 1970, it indicated that rich people are not as happy as some might expect. The study, funded in part by the Bill & Melinda Gates Foundation, set out to document the thoughts of people who had complete financial security, or something approaching it, in 2009. The organizers heard from 165 households, most with more than $25 million in assets, yet the majority did not feel financially secure.

They worried they weren't rich enough. The study revealed that even with fortunes exceeding $25 million, most people did not feel financially secure—they wanted just a bit more (see Reason No. 5). One respondent said he wouldn't feel comfortable until he had more than $1 billion socked away.

They worried they didn't deserve it, especially if they inherited money.

They worried their children might become entitled or aimless.

They worried that knowledge of their fortunes would change their relationships.

They worried about having a lack of purpose in life, or a job that is valued.

They worried about how to behave with people who are poorer, even if those poorer people are still fabulously rich by most standards.

They worried about how their fortunes could affect their love life, or their children's love lives.

When the study was released, Robert A. Kenny, a psychologist who counsels the rich and helped design the survey, told the *Atlantic*: "Sometimes I think that the only people in this country who worry more about money than the poor are the very wealthy."

All are legitimate worries, but an uncharitable observer might be inclined to say the rich worry so much because they have nothing else to do. It's true: many rich people keep themselves busy making money, spending money or giving it away, so they can keep the demons at bay. Many are workaholics (often itself a problem). Also, it takes time, education, study and knowledge to manage assets and run estates. But others don't need to work, don't want to work, don't have rewarding hobbies and can't muster the energy to give their money away responsibly, so life can get dull. What often eludes rich people is simply a sense of purpose.

They feel aimless, forget about what's important in life and descend into mischief or worse. They become bored, perhaps the most dangerous rich person's problem of all. Clay Cockrell, a psychotherapist in New York City with a lot of rich clients, says many have trust issues and worry about their purpose in life. "My clients are often bored with life and too many times this leads to them chasing the next high—chemically or otherwise—to fill that void."

American author Dotson Rader once summed up the problem during an interview for a biographical film on his friend Truman Capote, the legendary writer of *In Cold Blood* and *Breakfast at Tiffany's*: "The chief problem that rich people face is the endemic boredom of living in a social ghetto, because one class of people all think the same way, all who have the same desires, all who have roughly the same amount of wealth and they bore each other silly."

Capote, who spent much of the 1960s and early '70s socializing with rich people in New York City, was the life of their parties and even hosted a few. Finally rich himself, he became one of them, watching them, engaging them, amusing them—and finally writing about them. The article, titled "La Côte Basque, 1965," appeared in 1975 in *Esquire* magazine. Intended as part of a novel that was never finished, the thinly veiled account of the sordid lives of his high-society friends, with salacious details they recognized all too well, created a unique set of problems for his subjects and especially for the writer himself. Betrayed, every one of them abandoned him in unison, and he became bored himself, spending most of the rest of his life on the talk-show circuit, often drunk, in and out of rehab clinics, and making headlines for a series of less-than-flattering incidents.

Boredom is a particular challenge for youth. Parenting, whether you are rich or poor, is difficult. Teenaged angst is universal. Generation gaps persist. Youth everywhere find themselves in situations they regret. But for rich youth, it's apparently even worse. Studies show rich young people are more likely to have more drug and alcohol problems than poorer contemporaries.

Not only are they more able to afford drugs, but affluent youth may be tempted to use them to reduce the ailments—insomnia, anxiety, headaches, stomach issues—brought on by being over-booked into after-school activities, clubs and sports, and encouraged to be the best in all of them.

Despite being pressured to succeed, children in affluent neighbourhoods are just as likely as poorer ones to have parents who are unavailable physically and emotionally. Rich parents can bail their kids out of jail. They can pay for rehab. They can hire professionals. But in the end, all parents face the same anguish when it comes to their offspring, and often experience the same regret: they should have spent more time with the kids.

The challenge for the children of the superrich is often greater. They have had a pampered childhood and often have a skewed view of life. Some have an arrogance not yet tempered by age. But perhaps worst of all, they lack not only direction but any need to find one. All youth are looking for a purpose, but most find it through necessity—the requirement to earn money. Children of the superrich often don't have to work.

Documentarian Jamie Johnson, an heir to the Johnson & Johnson fortune, explored the question of how to avoid the dysfunction that afflicts so many rich families and their children in his remarkable 2003 film *Born Rich*. He interviewed his rich friends, most of whom regretted their decision to co-operate, and explored what his own future might look like. His father, a painter who has never had to work, agreed reluctantly to an interview, and suggested Jamie build a "collection of historical documents, papers, publications."

"As a career?" asked his twenty-one-year-old son, the filmmaker.

"Yes," replied his father.

"Collecting old maps seems pretty cool," Johnson would later tell viewers, "but I don't exactly see where the career part comes into it."

Money alone can't fix anxiety, depression, stress or loneliness.

And it can't fix the reason behind some of their problems: money itself.

Police blotters are overflowing with incidents of violence and vandalism perpetrated by some rich kids, and as always, the ones with famous parents get most of the ink: Cameron Douglas, son of Michael, went to jail for seven years for drug-related offences. Redmond O'Neal, son of Ryan O'Neal and Farrah Fawcett, went to jail for heroin possession. Many other celebrity children make headlines for lesser offences that would not be worth reporting if they weren't related to famous people (see Reason No. 1).

Some find themselves deservedly—and perhaps purposely—in the news for remarkably bad behaviour. Conrad Hilton III, brother of Paris and son of real estate and hotel mogul Richard, went to jail in 2022 for using drugs in violation of his parole, negotiated after a trans-Atlantic flight in 2014 in which he terrified passengers, abused flight attendants, picked a fight with the co-pilot, smoked pot in the bathroom, punched a bulkhead and yelled: "I will fucking own anyone on this flight; they are fucking peasants!"

Some youths grow out of that kind of behaviour and cringe at their youthful arrogance, but other rich kids are a burden to their parents long into adulthood. In the 1990s, John George Vanderbilt Henry Spencer-Churchill, the 11th Duke of Marlborough, spent untold sums to win a court battle to ensure his son, the drug addict and thief Charles James Spencer Churchill, now the 12th Duke of Marlborough, would never win control of his family's beloved 187-room Blenheim Palace and the surrounding 11,500-acre estate in Woodstock, Oxfordshire. But it was all for naught. The father and son apparently reconciled, and the son now runs the place. "My famous ancestor won the Battle of Blenheim in one day," the duke once told *Vanity Fair*, "but his descendants have been fighting it ever since."

Youthful troubles dogged Eva Rausing for most of her life. The fun-loving American daughter of a Pepsi executive met her husband, Hans Kristian Rausing, an heir to the Swedish inventor of the Tetra Pak, in a US rehab clinic in 1991. The couple had four children, mingled socially with royalty, were celebrated widely in Britain for their philanthropy, and jetted between their opulent mansion in London and a beachfront home in Barbados.

By 2008, Eva was arrested at the US embassy in London when cocaine and heroin were found in her purse, and in 2012, she died in bed as a result of drug abuse. At the time, her husband, himself an addict, couldn't bring himself to "confront the reality of her death." When he was pulled over two months later for driving erratically, police discovered drugs and mail addressed to his wife in the back seat. When they searched the couple's home, they found Eva's decomposing body, buried under blankets and surrounded by debris, still clutching the foil pipe she had used to smoke her last hit of crack cocaine. Rausing would later tell a hearing: "I took some measures to reduce the smell."

Life in the end wasn't much better for John Hervey, the 7th Marquess of Bristol, who inherited a fortune and died almost broke at age forty-four in 1999. Some say he was genetically predisposed to drug abuse. A few blamed his upbringing. His mother was absent, his father cold at best. Maybe he simply had too much money.

Hervey inherited £1 million at sixteen, and received another £4 million plus various properties at twenty-one, and went on a spending spree for the next two decades, selling off assets to support his lifestyle. Blessed thereafter with the traditional extravagances of wealth, including a yacht, a helicopter, a speedboat and a Ferrari, he descended into the excesses of the 1970s: binge drinking, shooting heroin and fulfilling his sexual desires with men and women around the world. "You can buy something that is self-gratifying," Hervey would say years later, "but self-gratification does not last long enough and it does not turn into happiness. I can tell you. I've tried it for a long time."

He moved from London to Monte Carlo to avoid taxes, then took up secret residence in Paris, before moving on to New York, where he hung out with Mick Jagger and Andy Warhol, among others, always in search of a new adventure. He eventually returned to Britain, living at Ickworth House, a sprawling estate that had been in his family since 1467.

The problem, for Hervey at least, was that the place had been partly owned by the National Trust, a charity for heritage preservation, since 1956. Hervey was restricted to a sixty-room wing of the main building as part of a ninety-nine-year lease. Often drunk behind the wheel of a car—and sometimes, horrifyingly, at the controls of his helicopter—Hervey terrorized an employee of the National Trust who lived on the estate, according to Marcus Scriven, who wrote the book *Splendour & Squalor: The Disgrace and Disintegration of Three Aristocratic Dynasties.*

When Hervey died of complications from drug abuse in 1999, Jessica Berens summed up his life in an obituary in the *Independent*: "In the end, he was just a junkie—scabrous, pathetic, helpless, desperate—in and out of court, almost penniless, usually friendless."

The luckiest grow out of youthful misadventures, and if they're rich enough, they can afford a lot of pricey help to get them through recovery: therapists, psychologists, psychiatrists, rehab clinics. For example, after the gruesome fate of his wife made headlines around the world, Hans Kristian Rausing apparently recovered, remarried and re-entered high society. Similarly, John Paul Getty Jr., son of the famous industrialist and father of the famous kidnapping victim, struggled with addiction well into adulthood but reformed himself and was later knighted for his philanthropy. He died at seventy in 2003.

Loneliness can affect everyone, rich or poor, but isolation is a common complaint of the rich. A 2016 study by Emory University in Atlanta surveyed almost 120,000 people, and indicated richer people are alone more often, socialize less and spend less time with family (but more with friends) than poorer people. It is just one study, of course, and there are many others, all with varying conclusions. But it's accepted wisdom that rich people tend to separate themselves physically from others, which also separates them socially. They don't necessarily need help, at least not from friends, because they can simply pay for it. They don't always read others well, and they often lack empathy.

Not only do some rich people lose perspective, they lose allies and friends, and often their sense of belonging. They become isolated, progressively segregated from the rest of the world, and it becomes ever more difficult to trust people, especially those perceived as different. They can't maintain relationships of any kind.

Like poor people, but for different reasons, rich people have trouble finding love, and they know better than most that money can't buy it. It's not that they can't find partners, lovers, husbands or wives; it's that they're never quite sure of what motivates their significant other, especially if that significant other is not rich. The actor Matthew Perry, for example, says he'll date only rich people, because he's been "burned a few times by women who wanted my money, not really caring about me."

Evalyn Walsh McLean, a socialite famous for being the last private owner of the infamous 45-carat Hope Diamond, who also somehow possessed the enormous 94-carat Star of the East diamond, had similar challenges. For the first half of the twentiety century, she was the queen of consumption, revelling in her celebrity, but it never seemed enough. Like so many other rich people, she became a lonely drug abuser who once wrote of her "pointless, pampered life of spending" and admitted that "money is lovely to have and I have loved having it, but it does not really bring the big things of life—friends, health, respect—and it is so apt to make one soft and selfish." She tore through her vast fortune until it was gone. Her children predeceased her. Her philandering, alcoholic husband was committed to an insane asylum. She died alone.

Many people—rich and poor—enjoy being alone, are comfortable in their own company, and, frankly, have had enough of other people. But for the rich and famous, isolation is not always the prettiest sight. The unpredictable billionaire Howard Hughes, one of the most famous recluses in recent history, is one example. A film producer, an aviator, an entrepreneur, a man about town, as a young man he was rich, dating movie stars, building and flying airplanes, sailing on his yacht and enjoying an inherited fortune.

He set a record for an around-the-world flight. He donated millions to biomedical research.

But he slipped into mental illness, sparked by obsessive-compulsive disorder. A germaphobe who was addicted to painkillers, he spent his last years holed up in hotel rooms, alone, naked and watching old movies. In the fullness of time, Hughes's reputation as a disturbed recluse overshadowed his various trespasses and triumphs.

Huguette Clark also took isolation to the extreme. Once described by the *New York Times* as an "antisocial socialite," she was born in Paris in 1906 and moved as a child into a 121-room mansion in New York City with thirty-one bathrooms, four art galleries, a theatre and a swimming pool. A painter, collector and philanthropist, she slowly receded from social circles by the 1960s. In the late 1980s, she entered hospital for a short recuperation and found the experience so much to her liking she decided to stay.

She had a team of hospital attendants with her at all times and employed a lawyer and an accountant to handle her legal and financial affairs. Various other staff, whom she never saw, meticulously cared for her three palatial homes—one in New York City, one overlooking the ocean in California, and another, a country estate, in Connecticut—though she never set foot in any of them for more than twenty years. The last two decades of her life were spent in hospital rooms from which she never emerged. Even in death, her executors protected her privacy, and perhaps theirs: "She died as she wanted, with dignity and privacy," her lawyer said in a terse statement after her death. "We intend to continue to respect her wishes for privacy."

Hughes and Clark are sad cases by most standards, but they may be among the lucky ones. They maintained control of their lives, or at least they appeared to. Their money couldn't solve their problems, they didn't have any friends, and they had little social interaction, but they were better off than others with similar afflictions and no money. They had financial power and apparent control the rest of us can only dream about.

But power and control are elusive and ephemeral. For many rich and famous people, their biggest fear is losing them. They get used to a world where money can solve every problem, until it cannot; where people will do whatever they're told, until they won't. Money can buy a better education. Money can mitigate legal problems. Money can save time. Money can help you acquire political influence, and even get you elected to public office. But money can't buy intelligence or knowledge or wisdom. It can't keep you out of jail if you've done something really stupid or evil.

And no matter how much you crave power, in a democracy, at least, it can't get you elected to office if you have no political skills, a reality that has frustrated rich people in the West for centuries. Hundreds, including failed US presidential candidates Nelson Rockefeller and Ross Perot, have proven that. And even when money does buy people entrance into political office, it can't necessarily keep them there. Donald Trump became US president because he had lots of money and a certain bizarre magic that enabled him to harness the attention of an unsuspecting media and a fed-up electorate. But maintaining that electability became difficult.

Loss of power or prestige or influence, especially when you've tasted it: there is almost nothing worse or more miserable for politicians and rich people alike. Having control is like a drug, and rich people forever need more of it. As Lord Acton so famously said, "Power tends to corrupt, and absolute power corrupts absolutely. Great men are almost always bad men, even when they exercise influence and not authority."

It's why so many politicians persist beyond their best-before dates. It's not an accident that Trump is publicly envious of dictators, who, like many rich people, have rationalized bad behaviour in their pursuit of power and convinced themselves they are beloved, often despite many indications to the contrary.

But clinging to power rarely ends well. In fact, that same power and money often make them targets of those who would take it away —the teeming masses of poor people. The rich and powerful hear the calls for economic equality. They see the crowds who attack the 1 per cent. They feel the social unrest. And they know it's coming. It is not for nothing that smart governments carefully monitor even the smallest protests, the most obscure demonstrations and the tamest rallies. They know, as do all rich people, that an apparent calm can turn into a storm in a matter of moments.

History is full of examples, and often it is the richest leaders who meet the most miserable ends. People simply don't like them. The hapless King Louis XVI of France, for example, started his reign in 1774 with the best of intentions. He had grand plans to reform government, abolish serfdom, remove the land tax that exempted nobles and improve the lives of his subjects, but rich people—the nobility—objected.

So while most of the country lived in hunger and squalor, the 1 per cent lived lavishly. At some point, Louis and his wife were so insulated from everyday French life they were unaware their appetites had grown out of control—the couple, and especially Marie Antoinette, had become synonymous with grandiosity, profligacy and exorbitance. By 1789, as the French Revolution began, their fate was sealed, and they lost their heads at the guillotine.

A similarly gruesome end awaited the equally hapless Nicholas II of Russia, a ruler with an affection for collecting too many Fabergé eggs, sparkling and ridiculously expensive knick-knacks that are the very symbol of modern opulence, while his subjects died due to privations, war and social unrest. After the Russian Revolution, he and his entire family were shot to death by a Communist firing squad in a gruesome surprise execution in 1918.

Romanian dictator Nicolae Ceauşescu and his wife, Elena, blithely built the sumptuous People's Palace, one of the largest buildings in the world, at a time when government-imposed austerity measures created endless hardships for Romanians, most of whom knew life was somehow better elsewhere. The happy couple were so detached from reality they didn't realize a rebellion was upon them until, in a now infamous 1989 speech, Nicolae addressed a crowd that turned on him with heckles and chants. Days later, the Ceauşescus faced a firing squad.

Mohammad Reza Pahlavi, the last shah of Iran, began his reign by instituting social, economic and political reforms, creating subsidies and land grants for peasants, profit-sharing for workers and literacy programs for the population. He used oil money to improve industry, health, education and the armed forces, and presided over decades of economic growth at rates that exceeded many other western countries.

But it all went south as the shah's reign continued. He conceived and supervised in 1971 what has often been called the most expensive party in history. To celebrate the 2,500th anniversary of the Persian Empire and show off Iran to the world, the shah built a huge tent city in the middle of the desert and invited everybody who was anybody in royalty and government from across the planet.

In an absurd display of hubris, the shah flew in famous florist Georges Truffaut from Versailles, accompanied by four hectares of soil, to create an elaborate and lush garden. Snakes and scorpions were cleared from the site, and fifty thousand songbirds, imported from Europe, were introduced. Construction of the tent city was supervised by a French company. The food came from Maxim's de Paris, considered the best restaurant in the world at the time. It was served on plates specially commissioned from a company in England and emblazoned with the shah's coat of arms.

In what the *Guinness Book of World Records* labelled the longest dinner in history, the bug-eyed guests scarfed down crayfish mousse, saddle of French lamb and quail presented inside peacocks, and washed it down with 2,500 bottles of champagne. It was all too much for the nation's struggling masses. The event is widely considered to have sown the seeds of Iranian revolution, and the shah's downfall.

Each of these rich and famous leaders—and many others—invariably found themselves rendered powerless—and widely despised—at the end. The rich people around them didn't fare much better as the reckoning began. Like tax evaders, Ponzi schemers, stock manipulators, inside traders, financial mismanagers and all manner of moneyed magnates, their wealth and fame, their status and power meant nothing in the end. Their money was worthless, their fame was little more than a liability, their power had evaporated, and their time had run out. As Bob Marley said on his deathbed, "Money can't buy life."

Conclusion

**Once, long ago,** I was awakened while sleeping, along with two fellow backpackers, on a beach along the Mediterranean Sea. A foot nudged me, and a voice in French told me to wake up. When I opened my eyes, two police officers were glaring down at me in the dark and said we couldn't stay there. It was illegal to sleep on the beach in Monaco.

"Go to France," they ordered, pointing to another spot on the beach perhaps a hundred metres away.

"We can sleep over there, but not here?" we asked.

"Of course," they said.

We couldn't tell the difference between France and Monaco, a magnet for the rich and famous since the 1950s. But I'm guessing residents of Monaco certainly could, even without a clear line of demarcation. And they weren't interested in having any poor student travellers in their midst. So we picked up our stuff and walked a few steps down the beach and went back to sleep.

Not all of the world's borders are so indistinct. Some are walled, some are barbwired. Others run invisibly over soaring mountains or through untamed rivers or remote forests, while a few bisect quiet private living rooms.

And some are just stark without any official division.

During a recent trip to Detroit, Michigan, I encountered the invisible wall between that city and the wealthy suburb of Grosse Pointe. It was like a slap in the face. Except for a discreet sign in a flowerbed, there's nothing official—and everything in general—to announce you are leaving one city and entering another. Or departing one world and crossing the threshold into another world. It's surreal.

On one side, empty lots and uncut grass, derelict buildings and demolished houses. On the other, exclusive parks, manicured lawns, lush landscaping, opulent mansions, private clubs and fashionable stores. It's sudden and it's striking.

"The border between Grosse Point and Detroit is one of the most shocking in America," says Bill McGraw, a journalist who grew up in Grosse Pointe in the 1960s and today lives in suburban Detroit. "It has become more pronounced over the years."

In fact, McGraw notes that Columbia University historian Kenneth T. Jackson mentioned the invisible wall more than three decades ago in his book *Crabgrass Frontier: The Suburbanization of the United States*, which described the border there as "the most conspicuous city-suburban contrast in the United States."

The two communities are more racially diverse today, says McGraw, but economically, it's only gotten more distinct. Grosse Point doesn't need shoreline police (though it has plenty) to tell poor people they are not welcome; it's obvious to everyone.

There are an estimated thirty thousand unhoused people in Canada, and almost six hundred thousand in the United States. Yet Canada has more than sixty billionaires today; the United States has more than seven hundred. The gap between rich and poor continues to grow around the world.

The wisest among us may not want all that money and the problems that accompany it, but we certainly don't want the troubles of the truly poor: living in a tent or a shelter, enduring cold and hunger, being assaulted, robbed, harassed or abused. Stigmatized, shunned. *Ignored.* Current rates of poverty in Canada and the US are shameful for a developed country in a modern world, but they are truly obscene amid the fantastic wealth and plenty that pervades our societies.

This won't stand. Not because governments will finally see the logic of a guaranteed annual income, or because economists, politicians or sociologists will come up with a solution to income inequality, or homelessness, or child poverty. Even if they do, globalization and political polarization will be obstacles to instituting reforms, says Walter Scheidel, author of *The Great Leveler: Violence and the History of Inequality from the Stone Age to the Twenty-First Century.*

Change will come about, Scheidel says, as it always has throughout history: chaotically as the result of an economic or natural disaster, a plague, a revolution or a really big war. "For six or seven decades from 1914 to the 1970s or 1980s, both the world's rich economies and those countries that had fallen to communist regimes experienced some of the most intense leveling in recorded history," writes Scheidel. "Since then, much of the world has entered what could become the next long stretch—a return to persistent capital accumulation and income concentration."

An oft-cited example is the Black Death, which ravaged Europe for five years in the fourteenth century, killing perhaps half the population of Europe and Asia. Much research concluded that it had far-reaching economic effects, creating a demand for labour and finally putting workers in the driver's seat. In many areas, demographic collapse shrunk the gap between those with money and those willing to work for a fair wage. Rents fell, wages rose, opportunities started to abound. Poor people could even buy property. The listing boat was righted, and all was square with the world again, at least economically—until it wasn't.

Other research indicates such effects are not universal or especially predictable. Sometimes, economic inequity is worsened by natural disasters because those with money are better able to withstand economic pressures. There's little doubt that the world changes after every famine, environmental catastrophe, pandemic, stock market crash, oil crisis or war, but by how much, where exactly and for how long? How long indeed, for no matter how many great levellers there may be, social and economic stratification inevitably begins anew.

After the 1929 stock market crash and the ensuing Great Depression, people were desperate for government to step in and cure the economic hangover left by the Roaring Twenties. Former US president Franklin Delano Roosevelt is still renowned (or maligned, as the case may be) for his historic New Deal, a series of financial reforms and regulations, progressive taxation and public-works projects during the 1930s that put the jobless back to work in a dark time.

As a result, wealth inequality during the middle decades of the twentieth century compressed. The poor weren't as poor and the rich weren't as rich. But as always, the spread began to stretch in the 1970s, and has been expanding ever since. Roosevelt's New Deal eventually gave way in the 1980s to US President Ronald Reagan and British Prime Minister Margaret Thatcher's commitment to deregulation and privatization. Unionization gave way to globalization. Political leaders everywhere became convinced that too much government and too many taxes were stifling the economy and making everyone miserable.

Unfortunately, this wasn't a raging success any more than the New Deal was perfect. Both worked until they didn't. During the financial crisis of 2008, many rich people were rendered broke (while a few became billionaires), but the gap between rich and poor has continued to expand since, and despite the apparent demand for labour in the wake of the COVID-19 pandemic, it persists.

And as long as rich people continue getting richer, it may be a while before it corrects itself. After all, wealth itself is the most powerful propaganda tool.

In 2007, George W. Bush acknowledged the growing gap between rich and poor. "The fact is that income inequality is real. It's been rising for more than 25 years." Little has changed since, despite the best efforts of some of Bush's successors. "The very rich are getting much, much richer while the middle class is falling further and further behind, and being forced to take on outrageous levels of debt," said Senator Bernie Sanders in 2022.

So what can we do?

We must first recognize that most of us are rich. If we have a place to live and food to eat and can acquire a passport, we're better off than millions of others. Like the multimillionaires and billionaires depicted in this book, we may not be as rich as we would like, but we are still rich. And we are not as poor as we are led to believe by marketing companies, influencers, Hollywood producers, our neighbours, the Kardashians and the media in general.

We could try to understand that money doesn't necessarily make us happy. It can and does make life easier, but only up to a point—and that point is not a million dollars. Once we accept that universal truth, born out by many studies, we can start thinking about what really matters. While really rich people are often happy, many are sad. And all of them will tell you that opulence and extravagant living rarely make things better, and often make things worse, a fact wise people have repeated for millennia.

The Greek philosopher Epicurus was one of them. Often criticized for advocating that humans should seek pleasure above all else, Epicureanism is often misunderstood. Epicureans don't seek pleasure the way hedonists do, through sex, drugs, rock 'n' roll or extravagant acquisitions; they define pleasure simply as an absence of pain. Pain can result from many things, including greed and envy, loneliness, isolation, lack of privacy, haters on social media and the hassles that inevitably come with possessions. More money and more fame can mean more problems, and more problems mean more pain. A simple life, with simple wants, with love and forgiveness, can lead to true happiness.

We can also change our attitudes toward those we perceive as rich or famous. Just because someone is rich does not make them smart. There are lots of rich people who are decidedly not, and lots of poor people who are brilliant. Neither do famous people necessarily deserve the attention—good or bad—they get, as any one of them will tell you. And while rich people don't necessarily deserve our admiration, most don't deserve our scorn either. Many are just as shy and uncertain as the rest of us.

We must open our eyes wider to the poverty in our midst and resist the temptation to avoid it on our travels—near and far. We can try to step across that threshold, break through the invisible wall. Being ignorant of the plight of others is no excuse for not doing something about it.

We can accept the fact that poverty persists in our communities because we have decided to allow it. We refuse, for the most part, to press our governments to introduce a guaranteed annual income or come up with other solutions, perhaps because we think it will give rise to a generation of lazy good-for-nothings. But we should know in our hearts and minds that most people, in fact, want to work. We also worry that such a move might cause wages to rise, and therefore the cost of goods and services to rise. And that doesn't sound like much fun, not necessarily because it will cause our economies to be less competitive globally, but mostly because it will cost more for take-out food and Amazon deliveries. We simply don't want to pay for it.

We need to elect governments that take wealth inequality seriously, that recognize it as a menace to our democracies, and realize that a nation where the gap between rich and poor continues to grow is an existential threat. This does not mean we should necessarily vote for left-wing or right-wing governments or anything in between, but we should demand a plan and stop tolerating such acute wealth inequality. The plan must bolster child care and education from an early age, to provide people with the skills they need to thrive.

We should vote for those who care about the entire population, rich and poor, not just those who are influenced by a few with more money than most. Not only is this the right thing to do, but it will lead to greater prosperity and a better future for everyone, rich people included, and avoid a chaotic outcome none of us wants.

We must demand more transparency from governments and public agencies on spending, deficits, tax policy, subsidies and government lobbying, and we should insist on better laws to prevent financial crimes and skullduggery, and urge stronger enforcement of those that already exist.

We can donate to organizations that fight similar fights. There is no shortage of them, and they are all looking for help.

We can volunteer to make the world better, to help others— and to help ourselves.

Finally, we can think about how much we have, and how much we're prepared to be content with. Rather than be envious of those with too much, is it worth considering if life just might be better with less?

ENDNOTES

Introduction:

p.2   *my father's last television appearance:* "RMR: Celebrity Tip with Pierre Berton," *Rick Mercer Report*, CBC, YouTube video, October 18, 2004, https://www.youtube.com/watch?v=MjYcPoGji20.

p.2   *J.D. Salinger:* David Shields and Shane Salerno, *Salinger*, paperback ed. (New York: Simon & Schuster, 2013), xiii.

p.5   *Bob Marley:* "Bob Marley interview about richness and money," *60 Minutes Australia*, Nine Network, YouTube video, 1979, https://www.youtube.com/watch?v=-GkyZr9VzPY; Rob Kenner, "The Business of Bob Marley," *Billboard*, February 4, 2011, https://www.billboard.com/music/music-news/the-business-of-bob-marley-billboard-cover-story-473231/.

p.7   *Philip Seymour Hoffman:* "Philip Seymour Hoffman on J.D. Salinger, Fame and Privacy," *Deadline Hollywood*, YouTube video, December 31, 2014, https://www.youtube.com/watch?v=7E5XMB8MZo4.

p.7   *George Michael:* Rob Tannenbaum, "George Michael Preferred Music to Fame," *New York Times*, June 21, 2022, https://www.nytimes.com/2022/06/21/arts/music/george-michael-freedom-uncut.html.

p.7   *Movie star George Clooney:* Miranda Bryant, "George Clooney: Twitter is stupid and stars using it are morons," *Evening Standard*, December 4, 2013 (from an interview published in *Esquire UK*, January 2014), https://www.standard.co.uk/news/uk/george-clooney-twitter-is-stupid-and-stars-using-it-are-morons-8982317.html.

Chapter 1:

p.10   *Douglas Fairbanks Jr.:* Ronald Bergan, "Obituary: Douglas Fairbanks Jr," *Guardian*, May 8, 2000, https://www.theguardian.com/news/2000/may/08/guardianobituaries.filmnews.

p.10   *Zsa Zsa Gabor:* Hillel Italie, "Jet-setting Hungarian actress Zsa Zsa Gabor dies at 99," Associated Press, December 18, 2016, https://apnews.com/article/entertainment-frederic-von-anhalt-us-news-ap-top-news-ca-state-wire-a0fdcb084fa44973b0b3e045d94f0062.

p.11   *Paris Hilton:* "That's Hot! Paris Hilton Inks Memoir Deal, Promises to Get 'Searingly Honest and Deeply Personal,'" *RadarOnline*, June 4, 2021, https://radaronline.com/p/paris-hilton-memoir-publishing-deal/.

p.12   *Bill Gates:* Alex Shephard, "Oligarch of the Month: Bill Gates," *New Republic*, June 4, 2021, https://newrepublic.com/article/162598/bill-gates-oligarch-month-vaccines.

p.13   *Jeff Bezos:* Amy Chozick, "How Jeff Bezos Went to Hollywood and Lost Control," *New York Times*, March 2, 2019, https://www.nytimes.com/2019/03/02/business/jeff-bezos-lauren-sanchez-amazon-hollywood.html.

p.14   *The Zuckerbergs:* Shawn Knight, "A rare look inside the personal lives of Facebook CEO Mark Zuckerberg and wife Priscilla Chan," Techspot, December 3, 2019, https://www.techspot.com/news/83011-rare-look-inside-personal-lives-facebook-ceo-mark.html; "Inside the home of Facebook CEO Mark Zuckerberg and wife Priscilla Chan," CBS *This Morning*, December 3, 2019, https://www.cbsnews.com/video/inside-the-home-of-facebook-ceo-mark-zuckerberg-and-wife-priscilla-chan/; David Roth, "Mark Zuckerberg Is TNR's 2021 Scoundrel of the Year," *New Republic*, December 22, 2021, https://newrepublic.com/article/164858/mark-zuckerberg-tnr-2021-scoundrel-year.

p.15   *Sarah Bernhardt:* Sharon Marcus, *The Drama of Celebrity* (Princeton: Princeton University Press, 2019), 14.

p.15   *stardom continues to evolve*: Owen Gleiberman, "Gigli," *Entertainment Weekly*, July 30, 2003, https://ew.com/article/2003/07/30/gigli-2/.

p.15   *Petra Ecclestone*: Maysa Rawi, "'Who cares about money?' Petra Ecclestone's mother says £12m wedding was worth every penny," *Daily Mail*, November 22, 2011, https://www.dailymail.co.uk/femail/article-2064722/Petra-Ecclestone-wedding-Mother-Slavica-says-12m-extravaganza-worth-penny.html; Helen Pidd, "Bernie Ecclestone tells court: £12m cost of my daughter's wedding was absurd," *Guardian*, November 10, 2011, https://www.theguardian.com/sport/2011/nov/10/bernie-ecclestone-denies-wedding-bill.

p.16   *fairy-tale marriage began to disintegrate*: Emma Pietras, "'I feel sorry for him': Bernie Ecclestone blasts Petra's ex-husband James Stunt over 'C-list celebrity dwarf' jibe," *Sun*, February 28, 2018, https://www.thesun.co.uk/tvandshowbiz/5688368/bernie-ecclestone-blasts-james-stunt-dwarf-jibe/; Amanda Cashmore, "There are children involved and there's no point slinging mud," *Daily Mail*, March 16, 2018, https://www.dailymail.co.uk/news/article-5511291/Tamara-Ecclestone-begs-James-Stunt-stop-criticising-family.html; Emmeline Saunders, "Petra Ecclestone and James Stunt's £5.5 BILLION bitter divorce granted," *Mirror*, October 12, 2017, https://www.mirror.co.uk/3am/celebrity-news/petra-ecclestone-james-stunts-55billion-11331137; David Jenkins, "The confessions of James Stunt—as his name makes headlines amid money-laundering accusations," *Tatler*, May 4, 2022 (from a 2018 interview), https://www.tatler.com/article/james-stunt-interview-exclusive.

p.17   *Burt Reynolds*: "A Look Back at Burt Reynolds' Iconic Nude Photoshoot in Cosmopolitan," *Cosmopolitan*, September 7, 2018, https://www.cosmopolitan.com/entertainment/news/a48108/burt-reynolds-cosmo-classic/.

p.17   *Lindsey Vonn*: Alex Passa, "15 Photos of Lindsey Vonn When She Thought Nobody Was Looking," *TheThings*, March 2, 2020, https://www.thethings.com/photos-of-lindsey-vonn-when-she-thought-nobody-was-looking/.

p.18   *Michael Jordan*: "Michael Jordan interview about gambling," NF2, YouTube video, October, 18, 2020, https://www.youtube.com/watch?v=clWuv4k51xo.

p.18   *Elin Nordegren*: Sandra Sobieraj Westfall, "Read the Only Interviews Elin Nordegren Gave about Her Split from Tiger Woods," *People*, May 30, 2017, https://people.com/sports/elin-nordegren-post-tiger-woods-split-people-interviews/.

p.19   *Jennifer Lopez*: "Ben and Jen Say 'Not Yet,'" CBS News, September 14, 2003, https://www.cbsnews.com/news/ben-and-jen-say-not-yet/.

p.19   *celebrity weddings*: Helen Bushby, "How do you keep a celebrity wedding secret?" BBC News, June 22, 2017, https://www.bbc.com/news/entertainment-arts-40367506; Alex Williams, "How Celebrities Keep Their Weddings a Secret," *New York Times*, August 15, 2015, https://www.nytimes.com/2015/08/15/fashion/jennifer-aniston-justin-theroux-how-celebrities-keep-their-weddings-a-secret.html.

p.20   *Kaitlyn Siragusa*: Kellen Browning and Kashmir Hill, "How Streaming Stars Pay the Price of Online Fame," *New York Times*, July 29, 2022, https://www.nytimes.com/2022/07/29/technology/twitch-stalking.html.

p.21   *Ava Majury*: Elizabeth Williamson, "A Child's TikTok Stardom Opens Doors. Then a Gunman Arrives," *New York Times*, February 17, 2022, https://www.nytimes.com/2022/02/17/us/politics/tiktok-ava-majury.html.

p.24   *Richard Fuld*: Lauren Tara LaCapra, "Unrepentant Lehman ex-CEO Fuld says firm 'was not bankrupt,'" Reuters, May 28, 2015, https://www.reuters.com/article/us-lehman-bros-fuld-idUSKBN0OD2MZ20150528; "Lehman's Fuld sold Florida mansion to wife for $100," Reuters, January 25, 2009, https://www.reuters.com/article/oukoe-uk-lehman-fuld/lehmans-fuld-sold-florida-mansion-to-wife-for-100-idUKTRE50P04L20090126; Brian Ross and Alice Gomstyn, "Lehman Brothers Boss Defends $484 Million in Salary, Bonus," ABC News, October 6, 2008, https://abcnews.go.com/Blotter/story?id=5965360&page=1.

p.24   *Joseph Cassano:* Laurence Fletcher and Lisa Schwartz, "'Man Who Crashed the World' Turns to Philanthropy, Real Estate," *Wall Street Journal*, July 2, 2018, https://www.wsj.com/articles/man-who-crashed-the-world-turns-to-philanthropy-real-estate-1530540000.

p.25   *Wayne LaPierre:* Mike Spies, "The Secret Footage of the NRA Chief's Botched Elephant Hunt," *New Yorker*, April 27, 2021, https://www.newyorker.com/news/news-desk/the-secret-footage-of-nra-chief-wayne-lapierres-botched-elephant-hunt.

p.27   *Haft family:* Kara Swisher, "Haft family feud escalates in new father-son fight," *Washington Post*, August 31, 1994, https://www.washingtonpost.com/archive/politics/1994/08/31/haft-family-feud-escalates-in-new-father-son-fight/c5719e70-1ed4-4458-a46c-904c17b1cb8f/; David J. Morrow, "Denouement of a Family Feud?" *New York Times*, June 20, 1999, https://www.nytimes.com/1999/06/20/business/private-sector-denouement-of-a-family-feud.html; Karen de Witt, "In Feud over Retail Empire, Family Splits in Public View," *New York Times*, August 29, 1993, https://www.nytimes.com/1993/08/29/us/in-feud-over-retail-empire-family-splits-in-public-view.html.

p.28   *Curtis Carlson Nelson:* "Carlsons' bitter family battle becomes public in court," Associated Press, May 2, 2007, https://www.mprnews.org/story/2007/05/02/carlsonfeud.

p.28   *Sumner Redstone:* "Family Feud," *Forbes*, October 27, 2007, https://www.forbes.com/forbes/2007/1112/108.html?sh=147b00ea28f0.

p.29   *Rudy Giuliani:* Andrew Kirtzman, "The Bromance of Donald Trump and Rudy Giuliani," *New York Times*, June 25, 2022, https://www.nytimes.com/2022/06/25/opinion/rudy-giuliani-donald-trump.html.

Chapter 2:

p.32   *Tim Blixseth:* Robert Frank, *Richistan* (New York: Crown, 2007), 77–78.

p.36   *Elton John:* The meltdown begins in the first four minutes of the 1997 documentary *Tantrums & Tiaras*, directed by David Furnish, available on YouTube: https://www.youtube.com/watch?v=1WeeozogBSE.

p.36   *the weather outside his suite:* "Elton John Carpool Karaoke," *The Late Late Show with James Corden*, February 8, 2016, YouTube video, https://www.youtube.com/watch?v=nblf7Yw4jys.

p.36   *it makes me shudder:* Ben Beaumont-Thomas, "Elton John: 'I can still explode at any moment,'" *Guardian*, October 22, 2021, https://www.theguardian.com/music/2021/oct/22/elton-john-i-can-still-explode-at-any-moment-i-just-have-terrible-feelings-about-myself.

p.36   *Naomi Campbell:* Cahal Milmo, "Naomi Campbell is accused of abuse—for the eighth time," *Independent*, October 27, 2006, http://www.independent.co.uk/news/uk/crime/naomi-campbell-is-accused-of-abuse-for-the-eighth-time-421832.html; Jess Cartner-Morley, "Naomi Campbell: 'Everyone has a temper,'" *Guardian*, September 7, 2013, https://www.theguardian.com/lifeandstyle/2013/sep/07/naomi-campbell-interview; Maureen Madden, "Naomi Campbell pleads guilty to assault," Reuters, January 21, 2007, https://www.reuters.com/article/us-crime-campbell-idUSN1618905320070116.

p.37   *loyal bitch:* "Naomi will be remembered for being a hard-working and a loyal bitch," dose, YouTube video, https://www.youtube.com/watch?v=BTo-wO4pO_Q.

p.37   *Nigella Lawson:* "We won the case but Nigella Lawson won the public's heart, say Grillo sisters," *Guardian*, January 7, 2014, https://www.theguardian.com/lifeandstyle/2014/jan/07/nigella-lawson-public-heart-grillo-sisters-fraud-trial; Jacqueline Rose, "Nigella Lawson, Charles Saatchi and the ugly face of patriarchal power," *Guardian*, December 20, 2013, https://www.theguardian.com/commentisfree/2013/dec/20/nigella-lawson-charles-saatchi-ugly-face-patriarchal-power-grillo-trial; Louis Degenhardt, "Nigella Lawson Tells Michael McIntyre Chat Show: 'I've had better times,'" *Guardian*, March 28, 2014, https://www.theguardian.com/lifeandstyle/2014/mar/28/nigella-lawson-michael-mcintyre-chat-show-interview.

p.38   *In 2016, Kanye West:* Shekhar Bhatia, "'I didn't hit on Kim!'" *Daily Mail,* May 5, 2016, https://www.dailymail.co.uk/news/article-3575074/Chippendales-dancer-turned-bodyguard-fired-Kanye-West-breaks-silence-happened-night-Met-Gala-calls-rapper-self-absorbed-person-s-met.html.

p.38   *Kardashian was later sued:* Diana Dasrath and David K. Li, "Domestic workers for Kim Kardashian West claim in lawsuit they weren't properly paid, given breaks," NBC News, May 25, 2018, https://www.nbcnews.com/news/us-news/domestic-workers-kim-kardashian-west-claim-lawsuit-they-weren-t-n1268488.

p.38   *Justin Bieber was sued:* Alan Duke, "Justin Bieber settles suit with ex-bodyguard who said singer hit him," CNN, February 4, 2014, https://www.cnn.com/2014/02/03/showbiz/justin-bieber-bodyguard-lawsuit/index.html.

p.38   *Britney Spears's former bodyguard:* Alan Duke, "Britney Spears downplays bodyguard's sex harassment suit," CNN, September 9, 2010, http://www.cnn.com/2010/SHOWBIZ/celebrity.news.gossip/09/09/britney.spears.bodyguard/index.html.

p.38   *Flores vs Spears:* "Fernando Flores, an individual, plaintiffs, vs. Britney Spears, an individual, Advanced Security Concepts Corp., a California corporation Does 1-100, inclusive, Case No: LC091061, Complaint for Sexual Harassment and Intentional Infliction of Emotional Distress, Superior Court of the State of California, County of Los Angeles," September 8, 2010, http://tmz.vo.llnwd.net/o28/newsdesk/tmz_documents/0908_brit_doc.pdf.

p.38   *Sylvester Stallone:* Alex Veiga, "Stallone Sued by Five Ex-Employees," Associated Press, November 29, 1999, https://apnews.com/article/135919bbb5645de94991531af5cb71b3.

p.39   *Anna Wintour:* Jerry Oppenheimer, *Front Row* (New York: St. Martin's Press, 2005), 24.

p.39   *Chuck Jones:* Maureen Orth, "The Heart of the Deal," *Vanity Fair,* November 1, 1990, https://www.vanityfair.com/news/1990/11/marla-maples-donald-trump-relationship; "Marla Maples' ex-publicist convicted in shoe fetish case," United Press International, February 16, 1994, http://www.upi.com/Archives/1994/02/16/Marla-Maples-ex-publicist-convicted-in-shoe-fetish-case/4878761374800/.

p.40   *Arnold Schwarzenegger:* Arnold Schwarzenegger, "IamArnold. AMA," Reddit, January 21, 2014, https://www.reddit.com/r/IAmA/comments/1vshw2/iamarnold_ama_20/.

p.40   *Gwen Stefani:* Rachel McRady, "Gavin Rossdale Cheated on Gwen Stefani with the Family Nanny for Years 'Right Under' Her Nose," *Us Weekly*, November 11, 2015, https://www.usmagazine.com/celebrity-news/news/gwen-gavin-cover-tease-20151111/.

p.40   *Christie Brinkley:* "Christie Brinkley and Peter Cook Settle Ugly Divorce Battle," CBS New York, June 25, 2012, https://www.cbsnews.com/newyork/news/christie-brinkley-and-peter-cook-settle-ugly-divorce-battle-in-dead-of-night/.

p.41   *Geena Davis:* Erika Åkman, "Tiffany Bowne comments on accusations made in Renny Harlin's new biography," *Ilta-Sanomat,* September 10, 2021, https://www.is.fi/viihde/art-2000008318915.html.

p.41   *Brian Wilson:* Elaine Woo, "Eugene Landy, 71; Psychologist Criticized for Relationship with Troubled Beach Boy Brian Wilson," *Los Angeles Times*, March 29, 2006, https://www.latimes.com/archives/la-xpm-2006-mar-29-me-landy29-story.html.

p.42   *Allen Iverson:* Kent Babb, *Not a Game* (New York: Atria, 2015), 176; Shaun Powell, "Allen Iverson and his persistent decision to be himself," NBA.com, March 25, 2022, https://www.nba.com/news/allen-iverson-persistent-decision-be-himself.

p.42   *Andy Warhol:* Guy Trebay and Ruth La Ferla, "Tales from the Warhol Factory," *New York Times,* November 12, 2018, https://www.nytimes.com/2018/11/12/style/andy-warhol-factory-history.html.

p.43   *Johnny Depp:* Eriq Gardner, "Johnny Depp Settles Blockbuster Lawsuit against Business Managers," *Hollywood Reporter,* July 16, 2018,

Misfortune and Fame

Misfortune and Fame

https://www.hollywoodreporter.com/business/business-news/johnny-depp-settles-blockbuster-lawsuit-business-managers-1127342/.

p.44   *Nicolas Cage:* Alan Duke, "Nicolas Cage caused his own financial ills, ex-business manager says," CNN, November 18, 2009, https://www.cnn.com/2009/SHOWBIZ/11/17/nicolas.cage.lawsuit/#:~:text=Los%20Angeles%2C%20California%20(CNN),his%20former%20business%20manager%20said.

p.44   *Billy Joel:* Patrick Macdonald, "He's Between Rock and a Hard Place," *Seattle Times*, April 13, 1990, https://archive.seattletimes.com/archive/?date=19900413&slug=1066235.

p.44   *Uma Thurman:* Zara Rubin, "Uma Thurman—in the throes of a custody fight with ex-fiancé—is also battling disgraced celebrity financial adviser Kenneth Starr over $2.5 million lost in risky investments," *Daily Mail*, January 10, 2017, https://www.dailymail.co.uk/news/article-4103020/Uma-Thurman-throes-custody-fight-ex-fianc-battling-disgraced-celebrity-financial-adviser-Kenneth-Starr-2-5-million-lost-risky-investments.html.

p.44   *Rihanna:* Joseph Ax, "Rihanna settles multimillion-dollar lawsuit with ex-accountants," Reuters, April 17, 2014, https://www.reuters.com/article/us-rihanna-lawsuit-idUKBREA3G24J20140417.

p.44   *Scott W. Rothstein:* Vic Walter and Mark Schone, "Scott Rothstein Gets 50 Years in $1.2 Billion Ponzi Scheme," ABC News, December 1, 2009, https://abcnews.go.com/Blotter/scott-rothstein-50-years-12-billion-ponzi-scheme/story?id=10868086.

p.44   *Tom Petters:* Associated Press, "50-Year Term for Minnesota Man in $3.7 Billion Ponzi Fraud," *New York Times*, April 8, 2010, https://www.nytimes.com/2010/04/09/business/09ponzi.html.

p.44   *Allen Stanford:* Department of Justice Office of Public Affairs, "Allen Stanford Sentenced to 110 Years in Prison for Orchestrating $7 Billion Investment Fraud Scheme," US Department of Justice, June 14, 2012, https://www.justice.gov/opa/pr/allen-stanford-sentenced-110-years-prison-orchestrating-7-billion-investment-fraud-scheme.

p.45   *Kevin Bacon:* Hadley Freeman, "Kevin Bacon: 'I thought I'd be sent to the TV graveyard,'" *Guardian,* May 20, 2017, https://www.theguardian.com/film/2017/may/20/kevin-bacon-thought-sent-tv-graveyard.

Chapter 3:

p.48   *Aaron Spelling:* Jeannine Stein, "The House of Spelling," *Los Angeles Times,* April 8, 1988, https://www.latimes.com/archives/la-xpm-1988-04-08-vw-1108-story.html.

p.49   *Beckhams:* Chris Riches, "Beckhams upset the neighbours with plans for a gym, wine cellar and cinema in £31.5 mansion," *Express,* March 31, 2015, https://www.express.co.uk/celebrity-news/567489/David-Victoria-Beckham-neighbours-object-to-London-mansion-renovation.

p.49   *five years later:* Amy Brookbanks and Issy Sampson, "David and Victoria Beckham at war with MORE neighbours—this time over privacy row at their £30m London home," *Sun,* June 11, 2020, https://www.thesun.co.uk/tvandshowbiz/11836958/david-victoria-beckham-war-neighbours-30m-london-home/.

p.49   *two months after that:* Laura Fox, "David Beckham 'wins dispute with neighbours over plans to boost security at £6m Cotwolds home,'" *Daily Mail,* June 12, 2020, https://www.dailymail.co.uk/tvshowbiz/article-8416353/David-Beckham-wins-disagreement-neighbours-plans-Cotswolds-home.html.

p.49   *mansion in white and red stripes:* Jessica Elgot, "Stripes on Kensington house are fun and here to stay, says owner," *Guardian,* May 12, 2015, https://www.theguardian.com/uk-news/2015/may/12/stripes-kensington-house-fun-here-to-stay-owner; "Court rules woman can keep her red and white striped townhouse," *Guardian,* April 24, 2017, https://www.theguardian.com/uk-news/2017/apr/24/red-white-striped-house-zipporah-lisle-mainwaring.

p.50   *Jason and Jodi Chapnik:* Vjosa Isai, "This Cedarvale couple sued for $2.5 million over a house they claim was designed to look like theirs," *Toronto Star,* October 5, 2017, https://www.thestar.com/news/

gta/2017/10/05/forest-hill-homeowners-claim-neighbours-duplicated-their-house-design.html.

p.50   *letter to the editor:* Jason and Jodi Chapnick, letter to the editor, *Toronto Star*, December 15, 2017, https://www.thestar.com/opinion/letters_to_the_editors/2017/12/15/letter-to-the-editor-from-jason-and-jodi-chapnik.html.

p.50   *painted their building bright purple:* Daniel DeMay, "Google Earth used to spite Sequim neighbors," *Seattle Post-Intelligencer*, July 18, 2017, https://www.seattlepi.com/seattlenews/article/Google-Earth-used-to-spite-Sequim-neighbors-11297479.php; "Purple garage upsets Olympic Peninsula neighbors," *Seattle Times*, April 13, 2009, https://www.seattletimes.com/seattle-news/purple-garage-upsets-olympic-peninsula-neighbors/.

p.51   *dildos:* Jon Wells, "Burlington neighbour dispute escalates to sex-toys-in-a-tree, makes Jimmy Kimmel show," *Hamilton Spectator*, July 13, 2022, https://www.thespec.com/news/hamilton-region/2022/07/13/burlington-neighbour-dispute-escalates-to-sex-toys-in-a-tree-makes-jimmy-kimmel-show.html.

p.51   *Detroit strip-club owner:* "Orchard Lake Man Erects Giant Sculpture to Flip Off His Neighbor," *Deadline Detroit*, November 16, 2013, https://www.deadlinedetroit.com/articles/7248/bloomfield_hills_man_builds_giant_statue_to_flip_off_his_ex-wife.

p.52   *an art installation:* Laurence Darmiento, "The feud over Bill Gross' lawn sculpture has come to an end. There were no winners," *Los Angeles Times*, June 20, 2022, https://www.latimes.com/business/story/2022-06-20/billiionaire-gross-chihuly-towfiq-glass-sculpture-laguna-beach; Sean Emery, "Billionaire Bill Gross calls for end to legal dispute with Laguna Beach neighbor, but hearings continue," *Orange County Register*, December 7, 2020, https://www.ocregister.com/2020/12/07/billionaire-bill-gross-calls-for-end-to-legal-dispute-with-laguna-beach-neighbor-but-hearings-continue/.

p.52   *Johnny Depp:* Jerry Oppenheimer, "Wild history of Johnny Depp's castle, which keeps luring nosy tourists," *New York Post*, May 2, 2022,

https://nypost.com/2022/05/02/wild-history-of-johnny-depps-west-hollywood-castle/.

p.53   *Zuckerberg:* Lucy Bayly, "Mark Zuckerberg Irks His Neighbors, Again, This Time in Hawaii," NBC News, June 29, 2016, https://www.nbcnews.com/tech/tech-news/mark-zuckerberg-irks-his-neighbors-again-time-hawaii-n601016; Christine Hitt, "Mark Zuckerberg dropped millions on even more Kauai property in Hawaii," SFGate, December 28, 2021, https://www.sfgate.com/hawaii/article/Mark-Zuckerberg-buys-kauai-land-hawaii-16732628.php; Maya Yang, "Mark Zuckerberg adds 110 acres to controversial 1,500 acre Hawaii estate," *Guardian*, December 28, 2021, https://www.theguardian.com/technology/2021/dec/28/mark-zuckerberg-110-acres-hawaii.

p.53   *Skywalker Ranch:* Norimitsu Onishi, "Lucas and Rich Neighbors Agree to Disagree: Part II," *New York Times*, May 21, 2012, https://www.nytimes.com/2012/05/22/us/george-lucas-retreats-from-battle-with-neighbors.html.

p.54   *Madonna estate:* Alun Rees, "Now any of us can ramble through Madonna's valley," *Daily Mail*, September 15, 2002, https://www.dailymail.co.uk/tvshowbiz/article-138353/Now-ramble-Madonnas-valley.html; Patrick Barkham, "Madonna loses fight to bar ramblers," *Guardian*, June 19, 2004, https://www.theguardian.com/uk/2004/jun/19/ruralaffairs.arts.

p.55   *air rights above the ground:* Ben Ryder Howe, "It's Public Land. But the Public Can't Reach it." *New York Times*, November 26, 2022, https://www.nytimes.com/2022/11/26/business/hunting-wyoming-elk-mountain-access.html.

p.55   *Mr. T:* George Papajohn and Steve Johnson, "Mr. T Chops Away at Lake Forest's Fiber," *Chicago Tribune*, May 22, 1987, https://www.chicagotribune.com/news/ct-xpm-1987-05-22-8702070954-story.html; Dirk Johnson, "Genteel Chicago Suburb Rages over Mr. T's Tree Massacre," *New York Times*, May 30, 1987, https://www.nytimes.com/1987/05/30/us/genteel-chicago-suburb-rages-over-mr-t-s-tree-massacre.html.

p.56   *Muskoka megaprojects:* Aaron Hutchins, "The battle for the soul of Muskoka," *Maclean's,* July 19, 2022, https://macleans.ca/longforms/the-battle-for-the-soul-of-muskoka/; Deborah Stokes, "Blight on the lake: The fight over a mega-cottage in Muskoka," *National Post,* September 29, 2021, https://nationalpost.com/news/canada/blight-on-the-lake-the-fight-over-a-mega-cottage-in-muskoka.

p.58   *Sean Connery:* Christine Hauser, "Actor and Neighbor Told to Stop Suing Each Other," *New York Times,* December 29, 2007, https://www.nytimes.com/2007/12/29/nyregion/29connery.html.

p.58   *Minnie Driver:* "Minnie Driver finally reaches settlement with neighbor over years-long driveway dispute," *DailyMail.com,* April 4, 2018, https://www.dailymail.co.uk/tvshowbiz/article-5578979/Minnie-Driver-neighbor-FINALLY-reach-settlement-driveway-dispute.html.

p.58   *Leonardo DiCaprio:* Associated Press, "Neighbors looking to sue DiCaprio," *Hollywood Reporter,* January 4, 2008, https://www.hollywoodreporter.com/business/business-news/neighbors-looking-sue-dicaprio-101805/.

p.59   *Dennis Rodman:* Jeff Gottlieb, "Rodman's Newport Party Pad Closes Up," *Los Angeles Times,* June 11, 2004, https://www.latimes.com/archives/la-xpm-2004-jun-11-me-rodman11-story.html.

p.59   *Madonna to trim a tree:* Penelope McMillan, "Judge Rules That Madonna Can't Justify Her Hedge," *Los Angeles Times,* December 7, 1990, https://www.latimes.com/archives/la-xpm-1990-12-07-me-6072-story.html.

p.59   *Val Kilmer:* Susan Montoya Bryan, "Kilmer apologizes to New Mexico neighbors," *San Diego Union-Tribune,* June 23, 2010, https://www.sandiegouniontribune.com/sdut-kilmer-apologizes-to-new-mexico-neighbors-2010jun23-story.html.

p.59   *Peter Nygård, Louis Baconfeud:* Kim Barker, Catherine Porter and Grace Ashford, "How a Neighbors' Feud in Paradise Launched an International Rape Case," *New York Times,* October 1, 2021, https://www.nytimes.com/2020/02/22/world/americas/peter-nygard-louis-bacon.

html; Eric Konigsberg, "The Billionaire Battle in the Bahamas," *Vanity Fair*, December 6, 2015, https://www.vanityfair.com/news/2015/12/peter-nygard-louis-bacon-legal-battle-bahamas.

p.61   *Yellowstone Club*: Much has been written on this subject, and all of it is fascinating, but Justin Farrell presents an interesting perspective and insider insights in his excellent book *Billionaire Wilderness* (Princeton: Princeton University Press, 2020), and Robert Frank writes extensively about Blixseth in his books *Richistan* (New York: Crown, 2007) and *The High-Beta Rich* (New York: Crown, 2011), both worth reading.

p.61   *Blixseth went to jail*: Jeff Manning, "Yellowstone Club founder Tim Blixseth jailed Thursday for contempt of court," *Oregonian*, December 18, 2014, https://www.oregonlive.com/watchdog/2014/12/tim_blixseth_claims_hes_too_br.html.

p.61   *Blixseth sued Montana*: Amy Beth Hanson, "Former billionaire suing Montana over forced bankruptcy, *Great Falls Tribune*, December 31, 2021, https://www.greatfallstribune.com/story/news/2021/12/31/former-billionaire-tim-blixseth-suing-montana-over-forced-bankruptcy/52146699007/.

p.61   *hall of mirrors*: Farrell, *Billionaire Wilderness*, 52.

Chapter 4:

p.63   *Anne Dias Griffin*: Jillian Eugenios, "This billionaire's wife wants $1 million a month after divorce," CNN, February 27, 2015, https://money.cnn.com/2015/02/24/luxury/griffin-billionaire-divorce/index.html.

p.63   *Nicole Young*: Liz Calvario, "Dr. Dre to Pay Ex-Wife Nicole Young $3.5 Million a Year in Spousal Support Amid Divorce," ET Online, July 22, 2021, etonline.com/dr-dre-to-pay-ex-wife-nicole-young-35-million-a-year-in-spousal-support-amid-divorce-169309#.

p.64   *"There is an art"*: Robert Frank, *The High-Beta Rich* (New York: Crown, 2011), 31.

p.65   *Mark Wahlberg:* Degen Pener, "The Most Talked-About Watches and Hollywood Collectors of 2021," *Hollywood Reporter*, January 6, 2022, https://www.hollywoodreporter.com/lifestyle/style/most-talked-about-watches-and-hollywood-timepiece-collectors-of-2021-1235069982/.

p.68   *Huntington Hartford:* Suzanna Andrews, "Hostage to Fortune," *Vanity Fair*, June 12, 2010, https://www.vanityfair.com/news/2004/12/hartford200412.

p.69   *Boris Johnson:* George Monbiot, "Boarding schools warp our political class—I know because I went to one," *Guardian*, November 7, 2019, https://www.theguardian.com/commentisfree/2019/nov/07/boarding-schools-boris-johnson-bullies.

p.69   *Upper Canada College:* James FitzGerald, *Old Boys: The Powerful Legacy of Upper Canada College* (Toronto: Macfarlane Walter & Ross, 1994), 335.

p.69   *Avi Lewis:* Ibid., 302.

p.69   *the coincidence is one of many:* Daniel Golden, "The Story Behind Jared Kushner's Curious Acceptance into Harvard," ProPublica, November 18, 2016.

p.70   *Lori Loughlin:* Kate Taylor, "Lori Loughlin and Mossimo Giannulli Get Prison in College Admissions Case," *New York Times*, August 21, 2020, https://www.nytimes.com/2020/08/21/us/lori-loughlin-mossimo-giannulli-sentencing.html.

p.71   *Scott Fitzgerald:* Dinitia Smith, "Love Notes Drenched in Moonlight; Hints of Future Novels in Letters to Fitzgerald," *New York Times*, September 8, 2003, https://www.nytimes.com/2003/09/08/books/love-notes-drenched-in-moonlight-hints-of-future-novels-in-letters-to-fitzgerald.html.

p.71   *Stephanie Ercklentz:* Jamie Johnson (director), *Born Rich*, 2003; "Stephanie Ercklentz, Chase Coleman," *New York Times*, January 16, 2005, https://www.nytimes.com/2005/01/16/fashion/weddings/stephanie-ercklentz-chase-coleman.html.

p.71   *Dollar Princesses*: Various articles on this subject are available in the newspapers of the day, organized by the US Library of Congress here: https://guides.loc.gov/chronicling-america-dollar-princesses/ selected-articles.

Chapter 5:

p.75   *Thomas Cooke*: William Chamberlaine, *The Life of Mr. Thomas Cooke, Late of Pentonville (A Miser)* (London: Law and Gilbert, 1814), 9. https://www.google.ca/books/edition/The_Life_of_Mr_Thomas_Cooke_late_of_Pent/hRFlAAAAcAAJ?hl=en&gbpv=1.

p.77   *J. Pierpont Morgan*: J.R. MacGregor, *J.P. Morgan: The Life and Deals of America's Banker* (CAC, 2019), 8.

p.77   *Rockefeller dividends*: Edward J Wheeler, "Persons in the Foreground," *Current Opinion* 45 (July 1908): 505. Accessed on Google Books.

p.78   *Jeffrey Winters*: Joe Pinsker, "The Reason Many Ultrarich People Aren't Satisfied with Their Wealth," *Atlantic*, December 4, 2018, https://www.theatlantic.com/family/archive/2018/12/rich-people-happy-money/577231/; Omar Ocampo, "An Oligarchy Expert Answers Our Questions about Wealth and Empowerment," Inequality.org, April 14, 2022, https://inequality.org/great-divide/oligarchy-q-and-a-jeffrey-winters/.

p.78   *Antonio García Martínez*: Alex Williams, "Why Don't Rich People Just Stop Working?" *New York Times*, October 17, 2019, https://www.nytimes.com/2019/10/17/style/rich-people-things.html.

p.78   *Roy Thomson buys newspapers*: Peter Day, "The life and times of a newspaper baron," BBC, April 1, 2016, https://www.bbc.com/news/business-35924027.

p.78   *"No leisure, no pleasure"*: "Lord Thomson Dies; Built Press Empire," *New York Times*, August 5, 1976, https://www.nytimes.com/1976/08/05/archives/lord-thomson-dies-built-press-empire.html.

p.78   *David Thomson rarely speaks:* FitzGerald, *Old Boys*, 256.

p.79   *Carnegie:* Andrew Carnegie, memo to self, New York, December 1868, http://www.shoppbs.pbs.org/wgbh/amex/carnegie/sfeature/meet_wrongpath.html.

p.79   *Trump fortune:* USA *Today,* "Millions, billions: Judge tosses Trump's lawsuit over his worth," ABC News, July 16, 2009, https://abcnews.go.com/Business/story?id=8100467&page=1; Dan Alexander, "The Definitive Net Worth of Donald Trump," *Forbes,* April 3, 2023, https://www.forbes.com/sites/danalexander/article/the-definitive-networth-of-donaldtrump/?sh=756a56fe2a8e.

p.80   *Trump used his charitable foundation:* Dan Cancian, "Donald Trump Forced to Sell Signed Tim Tebow Helmet as Trump Foundation Dissolves," *Newsweek,* December 19, 2018, https://www.newsweek.com/donald-trump-tim-tebow-trump-foundation-new-york-attorney-general-barbara-1264487.

p.80   *Warren Buffett:* Bill Gates, "What I Learned from Warren Buffett," *Harvard Business Review* (January–February 1996), https://hbr.org/1996/01/what-i-learned-from-warren-buffett; Fred Imbert, "Warren Buffett says the wealthy are 'undertaxed' compared with the rest of the US population," CNBC, February 25, 2019, https://www.cnbc.com/2019/02/25/warren-buffett-says-the-wealthy-are-undertaxed-compared-to-the-rest-of-the-us-population.html

p.81   *Warren Buffett on heirs:* Nicolas Vega, "Warren Buffett is 'halfway' through giving away his massive fortune," CNBC, June 23, 2021, https://www.cnbc.com/2021/06/23/why-warren-buffett-isnt-leaving-his-100-billion-dollar-fortune-to-his-kids.html.

p.81   *annual meeting of Buffett's holding company:* "Berkshire Hathaway Annual Meeting," *Nebraska Examiner,* April 30, 2022, https://nebraskaexaminer.com/2022/04/30/berkshire-hathaway-annual-meeting/.

p.81   *Charlie Munger on greed:* Tom Huddleston Jr., "Billionaire investor Charlie Munger: 'The world is not driven by greed, it's driven by envy,'"

CNBC, December 10, 2022, https://www.cnbc.com/2022/12/10/
billionaire-charlie-munger-world-is-driven-by-envy-not-greed.html.

p.82   *Warren Buffett on making a million:* Buffett has made this remark
or something similar numerous times; this one was at the 1995
Berkshire Hathaway annual meeting in Omaha: https://buffett.cnbc.com/
video/1995/05/01/buffett-rich-people-can-get-antagonistic-toward-
others.html.

p.82   *Catherine Zeta-Jones:* Jenny Davis and Julie McCaffrey, "Catherine
Zeta-Jones says she's had enough of being modest and won't apologise for
her fortune, looks and talent," *Mirror*, June 14, 2018, https://www.mirror.
co.uk/3am/celebrity-news/catherine-zeta-jones-says-shes-12707737.

p.83   *Money for money's sake:* "The Honor of Making Money for
Money's Sake," Simone Grace Seol, *Joyful Marketing*, podcast, episode 167,
December 14, 2021, https://www.simonegraceseol.com/podcast/
making-money-for-moneys-sake.

p.83   *Rappers burning cash:* Internet videos abound of this activity.
Reality is impossible to verify.
Trippie Redd: https://www.facebook.com/watch/?v=841261306977834
Run the Jewels: https://www.nme.com/news/music/run-the-jewels-
throw-money-burning-party-in-chaotic-ooh-la-la-video-2654848
DaBaby: https://www.facebook.com/watch/?v=495753118269194
Jon Geezy and Parlae: https://www.youtube.com/watch?v=NJhv6z5yk-w
NBA YoungBoy: https://ng.opera.news/ng/en/entertainment/
fc78ef61f462f396c3f26a8df122979b

p.83   *Carnegie promised to resign:* Carnegie, memo to self.

p.84   *The Giving Pledge:* https://givingpledge.org/.

p.84   *Bezos and MacKenzie Scott:* Megan Sauer, "Jeff Bezos makes a
long-awaited commitment to donate his fortune, while MacKenzie Scott
announces $2 billion in donations," CNBC, November 17, 2022, https://
www.cnbc.com/2022/11/17/bezos-says-charity-is-really-hard-as-scott-
gives-another-2-billion.html?

p.85   *she has signed the Giving Pledge*: Matt Durot, "Mackenzie Scott Just Announced That She's Donated $2 Billion to Hundreds of Groups over the Last Seven Months," *Forbes*, November 14, 2022, https://www.forbes.com/sites/mattdurot/2022/11/14/mackenzie-scott-just-announced-that-shes-donated-2-billion-to-hundreds-of-groups-over-the-last-seven-months/; MacKenzie Scott, "Pledge Letter," The Giving Pledge (website), May 25, 2019, https://givingpledge.org/pledger?pledgerId=393.

p.85   *Laurene Powell Jobs*: David Gelles, "Laurene Powell Jobs Is Putting Her Own Dent in the Universe," *New York Times*, February 27, 2020, https://www.nytimes.com/2020/02/27/business/laurene-powell-jobs-corner-office.html.

p.85   *girls are likely to be more prosocial than boys*: Isah Aliyu Abdullahi and Pardeep Kumar, "Gender Differences in Prosocial Behaviour," *International Journal of Indian Psychology* 3, no. 4 (July 2016): 171–75, https://ijip.in/articles/gender-differences-in-prosocial-behaviour/; Jolien Van der Graaff et al., "Prosocial Behavior in Adolescence: Gender Differences in Development and Links with Empathy," *Journal of Youth and Adolescence* 47 (2018): 1086–1099, https://link.springer.com/article/10.1007/s10964-017-0786-1.

p.86   *"Women overall"*: Tessa Skidmore and Charles Sellen, "Giving While Female: Women are more likely to donate to charities than men of equal means," *The Conversation*, https://theconversation.com/givin-while-female-women-are-more-likely-to-donate-to-charities-than-men-of-equal-means-141518

p.86   *"I plan to give virtually all"*: Bill Gates (@BillGates), "I can never adequately express how much I appreciate his friendship and guidance. As I look to the future, I plan to give virtually all of my wealth to the foundation," Twitter, July 13, 2022.

p.86   *Yvon Chouinard*: David Gelles, "Billionaire No More: Patagonia Founder Gives Away the Company," *New York Times*, September 14, 2022, https://www.nytimes.com/2022/09/14/climate/patagonia-climate-philanthropy-chouinard.html; Daniela Sirtori-Cortina, "From Climber to Billionaire: How Yvon Chouinard Built Patagonia into a Powerhouse

His Own Way," *Forbes*, May 20, 2017, https://www.forbes.com/sites/danielasirtori/2017/03/20/from-climber-to-billionaire-how-yvon-chouinard-built-patagonia-into-a-powerhouse-his-own-way/?sh=263a8c0f275c.

Chapter 6:

p.90   *Blane David Nordahl*: "Police Capture Cat Burglar Suspected of Striking Rich and Famous," Associated Press, October 17, 1996, https://apnews.com/article/ecbce9d64cd5d5a05c9c924267f2cdf4.

p.90   *Peter Scott*: Helen Collis, "Infamous Cat Burglar Peter Scott," *Daily Mail*, March 23, 2013, https://www.dailymail.co.uk/news/article-2298264/Infamous-cat-burglar-Peter-Scott-self-named-Robin-Hood-stole-rich-famous-died-aged-82.html.

p.91   *Gwyneth Paltrow*: Benjamin VanHoose, "Terry Sanderson Says Gwyneth Paltrow Case Was Not Worth It: 'I'm Gonna Be on the Internet Forever,'" *People*, March 31, 2023, https://people.com/movies/terry-sanderson-gwyneth-paltrow-ski-crash-case-not-worth-it/.

p.91   *Oprah Winfrey*: Sue Anne Pressley, "Oprah Winfrey Wins Case Filed by Cattlemen," *Washington Post*, February 27, 1998, https://www.washingtonpost.com/archive/politics/1998/02/27/oprah-winfrey-wins-case-filed-by-cattlemen/dd4612f5-ccbf-4e3d-a1c1-f84d1f4fd23c/.

p.91   *Jennifer Lopez*: John Woestendiek, "Jennifer Lopez sued for dog bite," *Baltimore Sun*, January 30, 2008, https://www.baltimoresun.com/bs-mtblog-2008-06-jennifer_lopez_sued_for_dog_bi-story.html.

p.91   *Miley Cyrus*: Kristi Oloffson, "Miley Cyrus and the Million-Person Apology," *Time*, March 10, 2010, https://content.time.com/time/specials/packages/article/0,28804,1970915_1970917_1970963,00.html.

p.91   *Jay Sommers*: Leah Chiappino, "Lottery winners' biggest downfalls from man who invested millions in meth to prize recipient murdered by lover," *US Sun*, July 29, 2022, https://www.the-sun.com/news/5891424/lottery-winners-biggest-downfalls-mega-millions/.

p.92   *Jack Whittaker:* April Witt, "He won Powerball's $314 million jackpot. It ruined his life," *Washington Post,* October 23, 2018, https://www.washingtonpost.com/history/2018/10/24/jack-whittaker-powerball-lottery-winners-life-was-ruined-after-m-jackpot/.

p.93   *William "Bud" Post:* Patricia Sullivan, "William 'Bud' Post III," *Washington Post,* January 20, 2006, https://www.washingtonpost.com/archive/local/2006/01/20/william-bud-post-iii/e2c64b90-550d-470f-8337-d853795888bd/.

p.93   *Jeffery Dampier:* "Guilty of murder, she gets 3 life terms," *Tampa Bay Times,* September 22, 2006, https://www.tampabay.com/archive/2006/09/22/guilty-of-murder-she-gets-3-life-terms/.

p.94   *Frank Sinatra Jr.:* Lauren Kranc, "The True Story of the 1963 Kidnapping of Frank Sinatra Jr.," *Esquire,* July 27, 2021, https://www.esquire.com/entertainment/a37106130/frank-sinatra-jr-kidnapping-barry-keenan-true-story/.

p.94   *Getty kidnapping:* Jillian Mackenzie, "The Tragic True Story of John Paul Getty III's Kidnapping," *Town & Country,* March 26, 2018, https://www.townandcountrymag.com/leisure/arts-and-culture/a9173861/john-paul-getty-kidnapping/.

p.94   *Theo Albrecht:* David Dawkins, "Billionaire Aldi Family Fortune to Hit German Court as Son Sues Mother for Embezzling Funds," *Forbes,* September 20, 2020, https://www.forbes.com/sites/daviddawkins/2020/09/20/billionaire-aldi-family-fortune-to-hit-german-court-as-son-sues-mother-for-embezzling-funds-reports/?sh=5e47ed94121a; Martin Childs, "Theo Albrecht: One of the two brothers behind the Aldi supermarket empire," *Independent,* August 14, 2010, https://www.independent.co.uk/news/obituaries/theo-albrecht-one-of-the-two-brothers-behind-the-aldi-supermarket-empire-2052354.html.

p.95   *Freddy Heineken:* Iain Martin, "Kidnapping Freddy Heineken: The Story of Europe's Largest Ransom," *Forbes,* September 27, 2019, https://www.forbes.com/sites/iainmartin/2019/09/27/kidnapping-freddy-heineken-the-story-of-europes-largest-ransom/.

p.95   *Li Ka-shing:* Mimi Lau, "Kidnapper of Li Ka-shing's son rang tycoon to ask where he should invest the HK$1billion ransom," *South China Morning Post*, November 29, 2013, https://www.scmp.com/news/hong-kong/article/1368203/kidnapper-asked-me-financial-advice-says-tycoon-li-ka-shing.

p.95   *David Letterman:* "Letterman Tot Kidnap Plot Foiled," CBS News, March 17, 2005, https://www.cbsnews.com/news/letterman-tot-kidnap-plot-foiled/.

p.96   *Jack Kent Cooke:* Lynda Richardson, "Yessir, That's My Baby: Redskins Owner Concedes Paternity," *Washington Post*, June 10, 1989, https://www.washingtonpost.com/wp-srv/local/longterm/library/cooke/daughter.htm; Michelle Green and Linda Kramer, "Baby Doesn't Make Three," *People*, November 14, 1988, https://people.com/archive/baby-doesnt-make-three-vol-30-no-20/.

p.97   *John Paul Getty Jr.:* Suzanne Adelson and Maria Wilhelm, "Paralyzed and Blind from a Drug Overdose, Paul III Is the Star-Crossed Getty," *People*, December 14, 1981, https://people.com/archive/paralyzed-and-blind-from-a-drug-overdose-paul-iii-is-the-star-crossed-getty-vol-16-no-24/.

p.97   *Steve Jobs:* Lisa Brennan-Jobs, "Growing Up Jobs," *Vanity Fair*, August 1, 2018, https://www.vanityfair.com/news/2018/08/lisa-brennan-jobs-small-fry-steve-jobs-daughter.

p.98   *John Lennon:* Elizabeth Grice, "'Dad was a hypocrite,'" *Telegraph*, April 1, 2015 (reprint of a May 23, 1998, interview), https://www.telegraph.co.uk/culture/4713954/Dad-was-a-hypocrite.-He-could-talk-about-peace-and-love-to-the-world-but-he-could-never-show-it-to-his-wife-and-son.html.

p.98   *Eddie Murphy:* "Eddie Murphy admits he fathered Mel B's baby," CBC, August 4, 2007, https://www.cbc.ca/news/entertainment/eddie-murphy-admits-he-fathered-mel-b-s-baby-1.692548.

p.98   *Joanne Whalley:* Bang Showbiz, "Val Kilmer in dispute over child support," CTV News, August 4, 2011, https://www.ctvnews.ca/val-kilmer-in-dispute-over-child-support-1.679194.

p.98   *Bobby Brown:* "Bobby Brown jailed over child support," Reuters, February 26, 2007, https://www.reuters.com/article/us-brown-arrest-idUSN2622244120070227.

p.98   *Dennis Rodman:* Associated Press, "Dennis Rodman must pay $500K," ESPN, December 6, 2012, https://www.espn.com/nba/story/_/id/8722062/dennis-rodman-found-contempt-court-pay-500k-child-support.

Chapter 7:

p.101   *Mike Tyson:* Mary K. Jacob, "Inside the Las Vegas digs Mike Tyson bought after years of money trouble," *New York Post*, April 22, 2022, https://nypost.com/2022/04/22/inside-mike-tysons-surprisingly-modest-las-vegas-home/.

p.102   *Wayne Newton:* Ken Ritter, "Wayne Newton moving out of Las Vegas home. Why?" *Christian Science Monitor*, June 6, 2013, https://www.csmonitor.com/Business/Latest-News-Wires/2013/0606/Wayne-Newton-moving-out-of-Las-Vegas-home.-Why.

p.102   *Debtors' prison:* Jill Lepore, "I.O.U.," *New Yorker*, April 6, 2009, https://www.newyorker.com/magazine/2009/04/13/i-o-u.

p.103   *Alex Jones:* Tiffany Hsu, "'Do these people actually think they're getting any money?'" *New York Times*, October 12, 2022, https://www.nytimes.com/2022/10/12/us/politics/alex-jones-denounces-verdict.html; Elizabeth Williamson and Emily Steel, "Sandy Hook Families Are Fighting Alex Jones and the Bankruptcy System Itself," *New York Times*, March 18, 2023, https://www.nytimes.com/2023/03/18/us/politics/alex-jones-bankruptcy.html.

p.104   *Toni Braxton:* Michelle Manetti, "Toni Braxton's Bankruptcy: Singer Admits Home Decor Obsession Lead to Money Loss," *Huffington Post*, December 3, 2012, https://www.huffpost.com/entry/toni-braxtons-bankruptcy-home-decor_n_2233458.

p.105   *Braxton:* Stephanie Gleason, "Braxton Bankruptcy Was 'Really Great' for Her," *Wall Street Journal*, November 9, 2011, https://www.wsj.com/articles/BL-BANKB-17708.

p.105   *Sonja Morgan:* Bruna Nessif and Beth Sobol, "*Real Housewives of New York* Star Sonja Morgan's Bankruptcy Nightmare Over, $9 Million Later," E! News, June 17, 2015, https://www.eonline.com/ca/news/667911/real-housewives-of-new-york-star-sonja-morgan-s-bankruptcy-nightmare-over-9-million-later-it-feels-great.

p.105   *The Chrisleys:* Kate Brumback, "Reality TV's Chrisleys get hefty sentences in fraud case," Associated Press, November 22, 2022, https://apnews.com/article/entertainment-business-sentencing-reality-tv-ccc146665477fd801bbf836504855d9f.

p.106   *50 Cent:* Jonah Engel Bromwich, "50 Cent Tells Bankruptcy Court Piles of Cash in Photos Were Fake," *New York Times*, March 10, 2016, https://www.nytimes.com/2016/03/11/nyregion/50-cent-bankruptcy-fake-cash-money-bills.html.

p.106   *Boris Becker:* Denis Campbell and John Hooper, "Boris Becker goes from boom to bust," *Guardian*, July 14, 2002, https://www.theguardian.com/world/2002/jul/14/tennis.sport.

p.107   *Becker as alleged attaché:* Reuters, "Central African Republic minister says Boris Becker passport 'fake,'" Euronews, June 19, 2018, https://www.euronews.com/2018/06/19/central-african-republic-minister-says-boris-becker-passport-fake.

p.107   *Becker goes to jail:* Andre Rhoden-Paul, "Boris Becker jailed: tennis champion sentenced over bankruptcy," BBC, April 29, 2022, https://www.bbc.com/news/uk-61276378.

p.107   *Patricia Kluge*: Geraldine Fabrikant, "Patricia Kluge's Third Act Is Sparkly," *New York Times*, April 7, 2017, https://www.nytimes.com/2017/04/07/fashion/patricia-kluge-jewelry-donald-trump.html.

p.108   *Trump stinginess*: Steve Reilly, "Hundreds allege Donald Trump doesn't pay his bills," *USA Today*, June 9, 2016, https://www.usatoday.com/story/news/politics/elections/2016/06/09/donald-trump-unpaid-bills-republican-president-laswuits/85297274/.

p.109   *Trump bills*: Emily Flitter, "Trump's art of the deal—dispute your bills," Reuters, November 13, 2015, https://jp.reuters.com/article/uk-usa-election-trump-bills-specialrepor-idINKCN0T215420151113.

p.109   *Trump bankruptcies*: Russ Buettner and Charles V. Bagli, "How Donald Trump Bankrupted His Atlantic City Casinos, but Still Earned Millions," *New York Times*, June 11, 2016, https://www.nytimes.com/2016/06/12/nyregion/donald-trump-atlantic-city.html.

p.109   *Leona Helmsley*: Enid Nemy, "Leona Helmsley, Hotel Queen, Dies at 87," *New York Times*, August 20, 2007, https://www.nytimes.com/2007/08/20/nyregion/20cnd-helmsley.html.

p.110   *Helmsley's dog, Trouble*: Cara Buckley, "Cosseted Life and Secret End of a Millionaire Maltese," *New York Times*, June 9, 2011, https://www.nytimes.com/2011/06/10/nyregion/leona-helmsleys-millionaire-dog-trouble-is-dead.html.

p.110   *Vijay Mallya*: Amie Tsang and Hari Kumar, "Vijay Mallya, Once India's 'King of Good Times,' Is Arrested in London," *New York Times*, April 18, 2017, https://www.nytimes.com/2017/04/18/business/vijay-mallya-extradition.html; "Kingfisher tycoon Vijay Mallya sentenced to jail in India," BBC, July 12, 2022, https://www.bbc.com/news/62131024.

p.110   *Carlos Ghosn*: Lisa Du, "What's Become of Ghosn as Nissan and Renault Revamp Alliance?" *Washington Post*, February 6, 2023, https://www.washingtonpost.com/business/whats-become-of-ghosnas-nissan-

and-renault-revamp-alliance/2023/02/06/16d061ea-a605-11ed-b2a3-ed-
b05ee0e313_story.html.

p.111 *John Jacob Astor:* Axel Madsen, *John Jacob Astor: America's First Multimillionaire* (New York: John Wiley & Sons, 2001).

p.113 *Sports team ownership:* Justin Birnbaum, "America's Richest
Sports Team Owners 2022," *Forbes,* September 27, 2022, https://www.
forbes.com/sites/justinbirnbaum/2022/09/27/the-richest-sports-
team-owners-on-the-2022-forbes-400/; David Cay Johnston, *Free Lunch:
How the Wealthiest Americans Enrich Themselves at Government Expense
(and Stick You with the Bill)* (New York: Penguin, 2007), 68.

p.113 *Willie Nelson:* Stephen L. Betts, "Flashback: Willie Nelson Settles
IRS Tax Debt," *Rolling Stone,* February 2, 2017, https://www.rollingstone.
com/music/music-country/flashback-willie-nelson-settles-irs-tax-
debt-196254/.

p.113 *Wesley Snipes:* Simon Hattenstone, "Wesley Snipes on art,
excellence and life after prison: 'I hope I came out a better person,'"
Guardian, November 2, 2020, https://www.theguardian.com/film/
2020/nov/02/wesley-snipes-on-art-excellence-and-life-after-prison-
i-hope-i-came-out-a-better-person.

p.113 *Sophia Loren:* Robert Wood, "Sophia Loren Jailed in 1974 Tax
Evasion, Finally Wins Case," *Forbes,* October 24, 2013, https://www.
forbes.com/sites/robertwood/2013/10/24/sophia-loren-jailed-in-
1974-tax-evasion-finally-wins-case/.

p.114 *Roger Moore:* "Sir Roger Moore defends decision to live in Monaco
and Switzerland," *Scotsman,* December 12, 2011, https://www.scotsman.com/
news/uk-news/sir-roger-moore-defends-decision-to-live-in-monaco-and-
switzerland-2480788.

p.114 *Sean Connery:* Associated Press, "Sir Sean: I'm No Tax Dodger,"
CBS News, March 6, 2003, https://www.cbsnews.com/news/sir-sean-
im-no-tax-dodger/.

p.114   *Phil Collins:* "Collins defends Switzerland move," *Express,*
September 24, 2010, https://www.express.co.uk/celebrity-news/
201547/Collins-defends-Switzerland-move.

p.114   *Lewis Hamilton:* David Tremayne, "'Fans, not tax, drove me
to Swiss exile,' insists Hamilton," *Independent,* November 6, 2007,
https://www.independent.co.uk/sport/motor-racing/fans-not-tax-
drove-me-to-swiss-exile-insists-hamilton-399139.html.

p.114   *The Rolling Stones:* Sean O'Hagan, "The Stones and the true
story of Exile on Main St," *Guardian,* April 25, 2010, https://www.
theguardian.com/music/2010/apr/25/stones-exile-on-main-street.

p.115   *Tax havens and Canada:* Alain Deneault, *Legalizing Theft: A Short
Guide to Tax Havens* (Halifax: Fernwood, 2016), 10.

p.116   *amount being moved into offshore accounts:* Ludvig Wier and Gabriel
Zucman, "$1 trillion in the shade—the annual profits multinational
corporations shift to tax havens continues to climb and climb," *The
Conversation,* February 23, 2023, https://theconversation.com/1-trillion-
in-the-shade-the-annual-profits-multinational-corporations-shift-to-
tax-havens-continues-to-climb-and-climb-200034.

p.116   *Panama Papers:* https://www.icij.org/investigations/panama-
papers/.

p.116   *Paradise Papers:* https://www.icij.org/investigations/paradise-
papers/.

p.116   *Pandora Papers:* https://www.icij.org/investigations/pandora-
papers/.

p.116   *Elton John, Julio Iglesias:* "5 Ways celebrities in the Pandor Papers
use the offshore system," ICIJ, October 4, 2021, https://www.icij.org/
investigations/pandora-papers/shakira-sachin-julio-celebrities-use
-offshore/.

p.117   *Hun Sen:* Clare Baldwin and Andrew R.C. Marshall, "Khmer Riche," Reuters, October 16, 2019, https://www.reuters.com/investigates/special-report/cambodia-hunsen-wealth/.

p.117   *Abdullah II:* Will Fitzgibbon, "While foreign aid poured in, Jordan's King Abdullah funnelled $100m through secret companies to buy luxury homes," ICIJ, October 3, 2021, https://www.icij.org/investigations/pandora-papers/jordan-king-abdullah-luxury-property/.

p.118   *ProPublica's "true tax rate":* Jesse Eisinger, Jeff Ernsthausen and Paul Kiel, "The Secret IRS Files: Trove of Never-Before-Seen Records Reveal How the Wealthiest Avoid Income Tax," ProPublica, June 8, 2021, https://www.propublica.org/article/the-secret-irs-files-trove-of-never-before-seen-records-reveal-how-the-wealthiest-avoid-income-tax.

p.118–119   *Peter Thiel, Ted Weschler:* Jesse Eisinger, Jeff Ernsthausen and Paul Kiel, "Lord of the Roths: How Tech Mogul Peter Thiel Turned a Retirement Account for the Middle Class into a $5 Billion Tax-Free Piggy Bank," ProPublica, June 24, 2021, https://www.propublica.org/article/lord-of-the-roths-how-tech-mogul-peter-thiel-turned-a-retirement-ac-count-for-the-middle-class-into-a-5-billion-dollar-tax-free-piggy-bank.

p.119   *Donald Trump taxes:* Russ Buettner, Susanne Craig and Mike McIntire, "Long-concealed records show Trump's chronic losses and years of tax avoidance," *New York Times*, September 27, 2020, https://www.nytimes.com/interactive/2020/09/27/us/donald-trump-taxes.html.

p.119   *Biden taxes:* Christopher Cadelago and Jennifer Haberkorn, "The Bidens made $579K last year, and paid a 23.8 percent tax rate, their returns show," *Politico*, April 18, 2023, https://www.politico.com/news/2023/04/18/bidens-tax-returns-00092675.

p.119   *"lose faith in democracy":* Jesse Eisinger, Jeff Ernsthausen and Paul Kiel, "When Billionaires Don't Pay Taxes, People 'Lose Faith in Democracy,'" ProPublica, February 28, 2022, https://www.propublica.org/article/when-billionaires-dont-pay-taxes-people-lose-faith-in-democracy.

p.119   *Ken Griffin:* Paul Kiel and Mick Dumke, "Ken Griffin Spent $54 Million Fighting a Tax Increase for the Rich. Secret IRS Data Shows It Paid Off for Him," ProPublica, July 7, 2022, https://www.propublica.org/article/ken-griffin-illinois-graduated-income-tax.

p.120   *"one of the largest private art deals ever":* Katya Kazakina, "Billionaire Ken Griffin said to pay $500 million for 2 paintings," *Chicago Tribune,* February 19, 2016, https://www.chicagotribune.com/business/ct-ken-griffin-pays-500-million-for-2-paintings-20160219-story.html.

p.120   *Elizabeth Warren:* John Harwood, "Elizabeth Warren interview," CNBC, December 16, 2019, https://www.cnbc.com/2019/12/16/elizabeth-warren-government-listens-to-rich-guys-who-dont-want-to-pay-taxes.html#:~:text=Elizabeth%20Warren%3A%20You'd%20have,t%20want%20to%20pay%20taxes.

p.120   *Koch brothers and political influence:* Tim Dickinson, "Inside the Koch Brothers' Toxic Empire," *Rolling Stone,* September 24, 2014, https://www.rollingstone.com/politics/politics-news/inside-the-koch-brothers-toxic-empire-164403/; Shane Goldmacher, "How David Koch and His Brother Shaped American Politics," *New York Times,* November 23, 2019, https://www.nytimes.com/2019/08/23/us/politics/david-koch-republican-politics.html; Alexander Hertel-Fernandez, Caroline Tervo and Theda Skocpol, "How the Koch brothers built the most powerful rightwing group you've never heard of," *Guardian,* September 26, 2018, https://www.theguardian.com/us-news/2018/sep/26/koch-brothers-americans-for-prosperity-rightwing-political-group; Jane Mayer, *Dark Money: The Hidden History of the Billionaires behind the Rise of the Radical Right* (New York: Anchor, 2016).

p.121   *Koch family feud:* Peter W. Bernstein and Annalyn Swan, editors, *All the Money in the World* (New York: Vintage Books, 2007), 252–56.

p.121   *Obama's inaugural address:* January 21, 2009 https://obamawhitehouse.archives.gov/blog/2009/01/21/president-Barack-obamas-inaugural-address. *Obama's second inaugural address:* January 21, 2013 https://obamawhitehouse.archives.gov/the-press-office/2013/01/21/inaugural-address-president-barack-obama.

p.122   *Koch-Buffett:* Henry Blodget, "Billionaire Koch to Billionaire Buffett: Screw Your Call for Higher Taxes—the Government Is Incompetent," *Business Insider*, August 19, 2011, https://www. businessinsider.com/charles-koch-taxes-buffett-2011-8.

p.122   *Adam Smith:* Adam Smith, *The Wealth of Nations* (Bantam Dell, 2003, originally published in 1776), 350.

Chapter 8:

p.123   *Bezos yacht:* Emily Burack, "Rotterdam Now Won't Dismantle a Historic Bridge for Jeff Bezos's Superyacht," *Town & Country*, August 11, 2022, https://www.townandcountrymag.com/society/money-and-power/a38973492/jeff-bezos-yacht-bridge-rotterdam-destruction/.

p.124   *Alex Rodriguez:* Maneet Ahuja, "Inside the Half Billion Dollar Fortune of A-Rod and J.Lo," *Forbes*, April 16, 2021, https://www.forbes.com/sites/maneetahuja/2021/04/16/inside-the-half-billion-dollar-fortune-of-a-rod-and-j-lo-how-the-breakup-will-affect-their-business-empires/?sh=2f5418287177.

p.124   *Lance Armstrong:* Juliet Macur, "For Lance Armstrong, Backing Down Might Have Hurt More Than Paying $5 Million," *New York Times*, April 20, 2018, https://www.nytimes.com/2018/04/20/sports/lance-armstrong-.html.

p.124   *Paul Manafort:* "Manafort, US government settle civil case for $3.15 million," Associated Press, March 5, 2023, https://apnews.com/article/paul-manafort-trump-pardon-ukraine-2016-campaign-f31b882c95793c34de7bb97233a8e794.

p.124   *Abigail Disney:* Sara McVeigh, "What It's Like to Grow Up with More Money Than You'll Ever Spend," The Cut, *New York Magazine*, March 28, 2019, https://www.thecut.com/2019/03/abigail-disney-has-more-money-than-shell-ever-spend.html.

p.125   *Disney documentary:* Brooks Barnes, "Documentary Critical of Disney, from the Disney Family," *New York Times*, January 23, 2022,

https://www.nytimes.com/2022/01/23/business/media/abigail-disney-documentary.html.

p.125   *Elizabeth Koch:* Brooks Barnes, "The Billionaire's Daughter Knows What You're Thinking," *New York Times,* February 23, 2023 https://www.nytimes.com/2023/02/23/business/elizabeth-koch-perception-box.html.

p.125   *Paul Piff:* Paul Piff, "Does money make you mean?" TED *Talks,* December 20, 2013, https://www.ted.com/talks/paul_piff_does_money_make_you_mean; Eric W. Dolan, "Researcher finds wealth shapes an ideology of self-interest and entitlement," PsyPost, August 24, 2013, https://www.psypost.org/2013/08/researcher-finds-wealth-shapes-an-ideology-of-self-interest-and-entitlement-19832; Marty Smith, "The Dynamics of Compassion," *Reed Magazine,* March 2017, https://www.reed.edu/reed_magazine/march2017/articles/features/paul-piff.html.

p.127   *Clarence Thomas:* Joshua Kaplan, Justin Elliott and Alex Mierjeski, "Clarence Thomas and the Billionaire," ProPublica, April 6, 2023, https://www.propublica.org/article/clarence-thomas-scotus-undisclosed-luxury-travel-gifts-crow.

p.128   *Rachel Sherman:* Rachel Sherman, *Uneasy Street: The Anxieties of Affluence* (Princeton: Princeton University Press, 2017), 21, 235.

p.129   *George Soros:* https://www.opensocietyfoundations.org/george-soros; https://www.georgesoros.com/.

p.129   *George Soros giving:* Rachel Sandler, "The Forbes 400," *Forbes,* September 27, 2022, https://www.forbes.com/sites/rachelsandler/2022/09/27/the-forbes-philanthropy-score-2022-how-charitable-are-the-richest-americans/?sh=12f3e074a098.

p.130   *Soros political influence:* Daniel Bessner, "The George Soros philosophy—and its fatal flaw," *Guardian,* July 6, 2018, https://www.theguardian.com/news/2018/jul/06/the-george-soros-philosophy-and-its-fatal-flaw; Emily Tamkin, "George Soros is trying to change the system that made him rich," *Washington Post,* July 6, 2020, https://www.washingtonpost.com/outlook/2020/07/06/george-soros-influence-excerpt/; Jason Silverstein, "Who is George Soros and why is he blamed in so many right-wing conspiracy theories?" CBS News, October 24, 2018, https://www.cbsnews.com/news/who-is-george-soros-and-why-is-he-blamed-in-every-right-wing-conspiracy-theory/; Kenneth P. Vogel, Scott Shane and Patrick Kingsley, "How Vilification of George Soros Moved from the Fringes to the Mainstream," *New York Times*, October 31, 2018, https://www.nytimes.com/2018/10/31/us/politics/george-soros-bombs-trump.html.

p.130   *Martha Stewart:* Brooke A. Masters, "Martha Stewart Sentenced to Prison," *Washington Post,* July 17, 2004, https://www.washingtonpost.com/archive/politics/2004/07/17/martha-stewart-sentenced-to-prison/5fa0d2aa-e936-4567-89db-168d7f7e1e18/.

p.131   *Conrad Black:* Paul Wright, "Interview with Conrad Black, Former Federal Prisoner and Millionaire Media Magnate," *Prison Legal News,* September 15, 2012, https://www.prisonlegalnews.org/news/2012/sep/15/interview-with-conrad-black-former-federal-prisoner-and-millionaire-media-magnate/; "Conrad Black through the years," CBC News, July 5, 2010, https://www.cbc.ca/news/canada/conrad-black-through-the-years-1.868133.

p.133   *Robert Fulford on Black:* Robert Fulford, "Schadenfreude: one of life's guilty pleasures," *National Post,* November 29, 2003, http://www.robertfulford.com/2003-11-29-black.html.

p.133   *William Randolph Hearst:* W.A. Swanberg, *Citizen Hearst* (New York: Charles Scribner's Sons, 1961), 488.

p.133   *Robert Maxwell:* Nicholas Barber, "What Bond villains tell us about the world we live in," BBC Culture, August 31, 2021, https://www.bbc.com/culture/article/20210831-what-bond-villains-tell-us-about-the-world-we-live-in.

p.134   *Rupert Murdoch, "ethics and integrity":* Dominic Rushe, "News Corp income rises by 12% to $5bn as Murdoch defends empire," *Guardian,* August 11, 2011, https://www.theguardian.com/media/2011/aug/11/news-corp-income-murdoch-defends-empire.

p.134   *Rupert Murdoch apologies:* "Rupert Murdoch at Leveson inquiry: 'I failed and I'm very sorry,'" *Guardian,* April 26, 2012, https://www.theguardian.com/media/video/2012/apr/26/rupert-murdoch-leveson-failed-video; John Plunkett, "Rupert Murdoch says 'sorry' in ad campaign," *Guardian,* July 15, 2011, https://www.theguardian.com/media/2011/jul/15/rupert-murdoch-sorry-ad-campaign.

p.135   *Nick Davies:* Peter Wilby, review of *Hack Attack: How the Truth Caught Up with Rupert Murdoch,* by Nick Davies, *Guardian,* August 21, 2014, https://www.theguardian.com/books/2014/aug/21/hack-attack-truth-rupert-murdoch-nick-davies-review.

p.135   *Rupert Murdoch secretly taped:* Jill Lawless, "On tape, Murdoch slams police investigation," Associated Press, July 4, 2013, https://apnews.com/article/2175ee4bfcad498fb2ccce82143c7987.

p.136   *Sacklers' wealth:* "Sackler family," *Forbes,* December 16, 2020, https://www.forbes.com/profile/sackler/?sh=46d0f2045d63. *Sackler history:* Patrick Radden Keefe, "Purdue, the Family That Built an Empire of Pain," *New Yorker,* October 23, 2017, https://www.newyorker.com/magazine/2017/10/30/the-family-that-built-an-empire-of-pain.

p.137   *testy exchange:* "The role of Purdue Pharma and the Sackler family in the opioid epidemic," House Committee Meeting, December 17, 2020, https://www.congress.gov/event/116th-congress/house-event/LC65831/text?s=1&r=10.

p.137   *Sackler family feud:* Joanna Walters, "Meet the Sacklers: the family feuding over blame for the opioid crisis," *Guardian,* February 13, 2018, https://www.theguardian.com/us-news/2018/feb/13/meet-the-sacklers-the-family-feuding-over-blame-for-the-opioid-crisis.

p.137   *Money considered dirty:* Alex Marshall, "Museums Cut Ties with Sacklers as Outrage over Opioid Crisis Grows," *New York Times,* March 25, 2019, https://www.nytimes.com/2019/03/25/arts/design/sackler-museums-donations-oxycontin.html.

p.138   *Nan Goldin:* Joanna Walters, "'I don't know how they live with themselves'—artist Nan Goldin takes on the billionaire family behind

OxyContin," *Guardian*, January 22, 2018, https://www.theguardian.com/artanddesign/2018/jan/22/nan-goldin-interview-us-opioid-epidemic-heroin-addict-oxycontin-sackler-family.

p.138   *Ida Tarbell:* Gilbert King, "The Woman Who Took on the Tycoon," *Smithsonian Magazine*, July 5, 2012, https://www.smithsonianmag.com/history/the-woman-who-took-on-the-tycoon-651396/.

Chapter 9:

p.141   *Winston Churchill and Noël Coward:* Paul Ferris, "The Fountain of Youth, Updated," *New York Times*, December 2, 1973, https://www.nytimes.com/1973/12/02/archives/the-fountain-of-youth-updated-with-the-cells-of-unborn-lambs.html.

p.143   *Jamie Lee Curtis:* Yasmin Gagne, "Jamie Lee Curtis is just hitting her stride. Here's how that feels," *Fast Company*, September 29, 2021, https://www.fastcompany.com/90674892/jamie-lee-curtis-is-just-hitting-her-stride-heres-how-that-feels.

p.144   *Ozempic face:* Amy Synnott, "Those Weight Loss Drugs May Do a Number on Your Face," *New York Times*, January 24, 2023, https://www.nytimes.com/2023/01/24/style/ozempic-weight-loss-drugs-aging.html.

p.144   *Justine Bateman:* Mike Sacks, "Justine Bateman Doesn't Want You to Call Her New Book Brave," *Vanity Fair*, April 9, 2021, https://www.vanityfair.com/style/2021/04/justine-bateman-doesnt-want-you-to-call-her-new-book-brave.

p.144   *Plastic surgery history:* J.P. Bennett, "Aspects of the history of plastic surgery since the 16th century," *Journal of the Royal Society of Medicine* 76 (February 1983), https://www.ncbi.nlm.nih.gov/pmc/articles/PMC1438692/pdf/jrsocmed00239-0074.pdf.

p.144   *Kaley Cuoco:* Lori Majewski, "Kaley Cuoco on Why She Doesn't Regret Any of Her Plastic Surgeries," *Women's Health*, November 24, 2016, https://www.womenshealthmag.com/life/a19924918/kaley-cuoco-plastic-surgery/.

p.145   *Kardashian Botox:* Adam Bryant, "Watch Kim Kardashian Get Botox," TV *Guide*, September 10, 2010, https://www.tvguide.com/news/kim-kardashian-botox-1022823/.

p.145   *Vaginal rejuvenation:* Dave Quinn, "'RHOC' Star Kelly Dodd Says Vaginal Rejuvenation Surgery 'Changed My Life,'" *People*, August 2, 2017, https://people.com/health/rhoc-kelly-dodd-vaginal-rejuvenation-changed-my-life/.

p.145   *Simon Cowell:* Clemmie Moodie, "I wasn't sure that I'd ever be able to walk again after breaking back in three places, reveals Simon Cowell," *Sun*, April 9, 2022, https://www.thesun.co.uk/tvandshowbiz/18218907/simon-cowell-bike-feared-walk/.

p.145   *Linda Evangelista:* Linda Evangelista (@lindaevangelista), Instagram, September 22, 2021, https://www.instagram.com/p/CUJZa4otWXC/?hl=en.

p.147   *Pam Behan:* Amber Goodhand, "Former Kardashian Nanny Tells All, Kris Jenner's Meltdowns & Bruce's Plastic Surgery," *RadarOnline*, July 13, 2012, https://radaronline.com/exclusives/2012/07/kardashian-nanny-tells-all-new-book-radar-exclusive/.

p.147   *Jane Fonda:* Paige Gawley, "Jane Fonda Wishes She Didn't Feel the Need to Get Plastic Surgery," ET Online, September 21, 2018, https://www.etonline.com/jane-fonda-wishes-she-didnt-feel-the-need-to-get-plastic-surgery-110166.

p.148   *RAADfest:* https://raadfest.com/.

p.148   *James Strole:* "From 'extreme fasting' to 'radical life extension', the dark side of body optimization," *Spark*, CBC Radio, March 22, 2019, https://www.cbc.ca/radio/spark/spark-431-1.5058858/from-extreme-fasting-to-radical-life-extension-the-dark-side-of-body-optimization-1.5058860.

p.148   *Dave Asprey:* Dave Asprey, "Biohacking: Why I'll live to be 180 years old," YouTube video, August 20, 2019, https://www.youtube.com/watch?v=7qJPf5O9kxc. Guy Kelly, "Meet the man who plans to live to 180 (and has spent $2 million trying)," *Telegraph*, January 22, 2021, https://www.telegraph.co.uk/men/thinking-man/meet-man-plans-live-180-has-spent-2million-trying/.

p.149 *young blood:* Lilly Dancyger, "Clinic to Offer 'Young Blood,'" *Rolling Stone*, September 27, 2018, https://www.rollingstone.com/culture/culture-news/young-blood-transfusion-new-york-clinic-730099/.

p.149 *"no proven clinical benefit":* "Statement from FDA Director Scott Gottlieb," FDA, February 19, 2019, https://www.fda.gov/news-events/press-announcements/statement-fda-commissioner-scott-gottlieb-md-and-director-fdas-center-biologics-evaluation-and-0.

p.149 *aldehyde-stabilized cryopreservation:* Robert L. McIntyre and Gregory M. Fahy, "Aldehyde-stabilized cryopreservation," *Cryobiology* 71, no. 3 (December 2015), https://pubmed.ncbi.nlm.nih.gov/26408851/; Sharon Begley, "After ghoulish allegations, a brain-preservation company seeks redemption," STAT News, January 30, 2019, https://www.statnews.com/2019/01/30/nectome-brain-preservation-redemption/.

p.149 *Yuval Noah Harari:* Yuval Noah Harari, *Homo Deus: A Brief History of Tomorrow* (Toronto: Signal, 2015), 23.

p.150 *When the rich set their sights:* Ian Sample, "If they could turn back time: how tech billionaires are trying to reverse the ageing process," *Guardian*, February 17, 2022, https://www.theguardian.com/science/2022/feb/17/if-they-could-turn-back-time-how-tech-billionaires-are-trying-to-reverse-the-ageing-process.

p.150 *Silicon Valley hotbed:* Tad Friend, "Silicon Valley's Quest to Live Forever," *New Yorker*, March 17, 2017, https://www.newyorker.com/magazine/2017/04/03/silicon-valleys-quest-to-live-forever.

p.150 *attention of billionaires:* Michael Shermer, "Radical Life-Extension Is Not around the Corner," *Scientific American*, October 1, 2016, https://www.scientificamerican.com/article/radical-life-extension-is-not-around-the-corner/.

p.150   *Calico:* https://www.calicolabs.com/.

p.150   *Unity Biotecnology, Bezos:* Andrew Zaleski, "Why Jeff Bezos is back-ing this Silicon Valley scientist who is working on a cure for aging," CNBC, August 29, 2018, https://www.cnbc.com/2018/08/29/jeff-bezos-backs-silicon-valley-scientist-working-on-a-cure-for-aging.html.

p.150   *Adam Leith Gollner:* Adam Leith Gollner, *The Book of Immortality: The Science, Belief, and Magic Behind Living Forever* (New York: Scribner, 2013), 363.

p.151   *Thiel, Methuselah:* "PayPal Co-Founder Pledges $3.5 Million to Methuselah Foundation," *Philanthropy News Digest*, September 30, 2006, https://philanthropynewsdigest.org/news/paypal-co-founder-pledges-3.5-million-to-methuselah-foundation.

p.151   *Thiel, Alcor:* "Peter Thiel pledges $3.5 Million to antiaging research," Alcor, September 19, 2006, https://www.alcor.org/2006/09/peter_thiel_pledges_35_million/.

p.151   *Bill Gates:* Bill Gates, "Ask Me Anything," Reddit, https://www.reddit.com/r/IAmA/comments/2tzjp7/hi_reddit_im_bill_gates_and_im_back_for_my_third/; Ina Fried, "Bill Gates Worries about Machines Gaining Super Intelligence," *Vox*, January 28, 2015, https://www.vox.com/2015/1/28/11558204/bill-gates-worries-about-machines-gaining-super-intelligence.

p.151   *Michael Shermer:* Michael Shermer, *Heavens on Earth: The Scientific Search for the Afterlife, Immortality, and Utopia* (New York: Henry Holt, 2018), 232.

p.153   *Luxury bunkers:* Michelle Butterfield, "Surviving in style: Canadian demand for luxury bunkers through the roof," Global News, April 2, 2022, https://globalnews.ca/news/8728927/bunkers-fallout-shelters-canada-demand/.

p.153   *Guy Laliberté:* Élizabeth Ménard, "Le nouveau cirque de Guy Laliberté: L'atoll de Nukutepipi," *Journal de Montréal*, April 25, 2015,

https://www.journaldemontreal.com/2015/04/25/le-nouveau-cirque-de-guy-laliberte-latoll-de-nukutepipi.

p.153   *charged for cannabis:* "Cirque du Soleil's founder charged with cannabis offences in French Polynesia," CBC News, November 13, 2019, https://www.cbc.ca/news/canada/montreal/cirque-du-soleil-cannabis-1.5357494.

p.153   *Peter Thiel in New Zealand:* Mark O'Connell, "Why Silicon Valley billionaires are preparing for the apocalypse in New Zealand," *Guardian,* February 15, 2018, https://www.theguardian.com/news/2018/feb/15/why-silicon-valley-billionaires-are-prepping-for-the-apocalypse-in-new-zealand; Ryan Mac, "The Many Contradictions of Peter Thiel's New Zealand Citizenship," *Forbes,* February 1, 2017, https://www.forbes.com/sites/ryanmac/2017/02/01/the-many-contradictions-of-peter-thiels-new-zealand-citizenship/?sh=3d2347bc1317; Tess McClure, "Billionaire Peter Thiel refused consent for sprawling lodge in New Zealand," *Guardian,* August 18, 2022, https://www.theguardian.com/technology/2022/aug/18/peter-thiel-refused-consent-for-sprawling-lodge-in-new-zealand-local-council.

p.154   *Anthony Burgess:* Anthony Burgess, *A Clockwork Orange* (London: Penguin, 1972, first published by William Heinemann, 1962), 9. The note Burgess wrote in the margin is on the manuscript at the McMaster University Library Archives: https://library.mcmaster.ca/archives/b/burgess.01.htm.

p.155   *Pierre Berton Show guests:* A partial list of guests on the show can be found in the Pierre Berton fonds at the McMaster University Library: https://library.mcmaster.ca/finding-aid/berton.

p.156   *Susan Strasberg:* Tom Vallance, "Obituary: Susan Strasberg," *Independent,* January 25, 1999, https://www.independent.co.uk/arts-entertainment/obituary-susan-strasberg-1076156.html.

p.156   *Barbara Feldon:* Jim Clash, "Barbara Feldon (Agent 99): Living Alone in New York, and Loving It!" *Forbes,* March 27, 2016, https://www.forbes.com/sites/jimclash/2016/03/27/barbara-feldon-agent-99-living-alone-in-new-york-and-loving-it/?sh=27f21a784d1e.

p.156   Time's list: "The TIME 100 Persons of the Century," *Time*, June 6, 1999, https://content.time.com/time/magazine/article/0,9171,26473,00.html.

Chapter 10:

p.160   *Michael Rockefeller:* Leslie Trew Magraw, "Kickstart an Age-Old Mystery," *National Geographic*, September 12, 2012, https://www.nationalgeographic.com/travel/article/kickstart-an-age-old-mystery.

p.161   *Sandy Pittman:* "Storm over Everest," *Frontline*, PBS, https://www.pbs.org/wgbh/pages/frontline/everest/stories/media.html.

p.162   *The Joys and Dilemmas of Wealth:* Graeme Wood, "Secret Fears of the Super-Rich," *Atlantic*, April 15, 2011, https://www.theatlantic.com/magazine/archive/2011/04/secret-fears-of-the-super-rich/308419/.

p.163   *Dotson Rader on Capote:* Ebs Burnough, *The Capote Tapes*, TVO Today Docs, YouTube video, https://www.youtube.com/watch?v=7OR8hTpCLog.

p.165   *Jamie Johnson:* Johnson, *Born Rich*.

p.165   *Cameron Douglas:* Dave Itzkoff, "The Life of Cameron Douglas, from Privilege to Prison and Back," *New York Times*, October 19, 2019, https://www.nytimes.com/2019/10/19/books/cameron-douglas-long-way-home.html.

p.165   *Redmond O'Neal:* Alexia Fernández, "Redmond O'Neal Blames Arrest on Parents Ryan and Farrah Fawcett: 'I Never Wanted Attention,'" *People*, May 31, 2018, https://people.com/movies/redmond-oneal-blames-arrest-on-famous-parents/.

p.166   *Conrad Hilton III:* Aili Nahas, "The Hiltons Are 'Disappointed' but Not 'Surprised' by Conrad's Parole Violation, Jail Sentence: He 'Has Had a Drug Problem for Years,'" *People*, June 7, 2016, https://people.com/crime/conrad-hilton-in-prison-family-not-surprised/.

p.166   *Conrad Hilton flight:* Amy Wallace, "Conrad Hilton and the Terrible, Horrible No Good, Very Bad Flight," GQ, March 2, 2015, https://www.gq.com/story/conrad-hilton-investigation.

p.166   *Blenheim Palace:* James Reginato, "The Duke of Marlborough, Savior of Blenheim Palace, Has Died at Age 88," *Vanity Fair,* October 18, 2014, https://www.vanityfair.com/style/2014/10/duke-of-marlborough-died-at-age-88.

p.166   *Eva Rausing:* Dan Bilefsky, "A Wealthy Family's Battle with Drugs Laid Bare, but to What End?" *New York Times,* August 11, 2017, https://www.nytimes.com/2017/08/11/books/a-wealthy-familys-battle-with-drugs-laid-bare-but-to-what-end.html.

p.167   *John Hervey:* Anthony Haden-Guest, "The end of the peer," *Guardian,* January 22, 2006, https://www.theguardian.com/theobserver/2006/jan/22/features.magazine37.

p.167   *John Hervey on self-gratification:* Jessica Berens, "Obituary: The Marquess of Bristol," *Independent,* January 12, 1999, https://www.independent.co.uk/arts-entertainment/obituary-the-marquess-of-bristol-1046531.html.

p.168   *Hans Kristian Rausing:* Guy Walters, "How the billionaire who hid his wife's dead body schmoozed his way back into society," *Daily Mail,* January 6, 2017, https://www.dailymail.co.uk/news/article-4096442/How-billionaire-hid-wife-s-dead-body-schmoozed-way-society-Tetra-Pak-heir-s-incredible-social-resurrection-ditching-drugs-marrying-Establishment-arm-candy-generous-wealth.html.

p.169   *Matthew Perry:* Deirde Simonds and Rebecca Davison, "Matthew Perry recalls being 'burned a few times by women who wanted' his money in past relationships," *Daily Mail,* October 20, 2022, https://www.dailymail.co.uk/tvshowbiz/article-11338843/Matthew-Perry-recalls-burned-times-women-wanted-money-not-just-love.html.

p.169   *Evalyn Walsh McLean:* Evalyn Walsh McLean, *Father Struck It Rich* (Boston: Little, Brown and Company, 1935), 308.

p.169   *Howard Hughes:* Michael Drosnin, *Citizen Hughes* (New York: Holt, Rinehart and Winston, 1985), 455–57.

p.170   *Huguette Clark:* Margalit Fox, "Huguette Clark, Reclusive Heiress, Dies at 104," *New York Times,* May 24, 2011, https://www.nytimes.com/ 2011/05/25/nyregion/huguette-clark-recluse-heiress-dies-at-104.html.

Conclusion:

p.176   *Bill McGraw:* Interview with author, February 27, 2023.

p.177   *Walter Scheidel:* Walter Scheidel, "Can inequality only be fixed by war, revolution or plague?" *Economist,* September 10, 2018, https://www. economist.com/open-future/2018/09/10/can-inequality-only-be-fixed- by-war-revolution-or-plague.

p.177   *Inequality in history:* Bas van Bavel and Marten Scheffer, "Historical effects of shocks on inequality: the great leveler revisited," *Humanities and Social Sciences Communications* 8, no. 76 (2021), https://doi.org/ 10.1057/s41599-021-00763-4.

p.179   *George W. Bush:* Michael Abramowitz and Lori Montgomery, "Bush Addresses Income Inequality in Economic Speech Touches on Executive Pay as Senators Move to Rein It In," *Washington Post,* February 1, 2007, https://www.washingtonpost.com/archive/ politics/2007/02/01/bush-addresses-income-inequality-span- classbankheadeconomic-speech-touches-on-executive-pay-as- senators- move-to-rein-it-inspan/c8904217-19cc-4b9e-a3f5- bf41834e7bd2/.

p.179   *Bernie Sanders:* "Rich Got Richer While Middle Class Took on More Debt and Fell Further Behind," Bernie Sanders website, September 28, 2022, https://www.sanders.senate.gov/press-releases/ news-rich-got-richer-while-middle-class-took-on-more-debt- and-fell-further-behind-according-to-new-cbo-report/.

ACKNOWLEDGEMENTS

Most rich people are reluctant to share details about their wealth. Those who come into money suddenly are sometimes exceptions, but they learn to be discreet soon enough. And nobody, rich or poor, is enthusiastic about having the public know about their problems. So I am grateful for all those who have shared, willingly or not, their troubles related to fortune and fame, and the many writers and journalists who have documented their travails over the years.

I am grateful to Teresa Evans, who read an early version of the manuscript and guided me away from endless trespasses. Peter Norman helped focus the book, and improved pace, wording, flow and structure, and once again persuaded me to get rid of some unnecessary stuff. Caroline Skelton went through the manuscript with her usual watchful eye, sharpening the language, cutting excess and sparing me from many embarrassments or inaccuracies. Finally, I am beholden to Anna Comfort O'Keeffe, publisher at Douglas & McIntyre, who, as always, has been an enthusiastic partner.

INDEX